REMEMBER THE ALAMO!

andmark
BOOKS

REMEMBER THE ALAMO!

Robert Penn Warren

Illustrated by William Moyers

RANDOM HOUSE • NEW YORK

To Gabriel

Contents

REMEMBER THE ALAMO!

1

How the Alamo
Got Its Name

THE STORY OF THE ALAMO IS A STORY OF COURAGE. IT IS a story of the simplest kind of courage—of a bitter and unflinching fight against overwhelming odds, to the last man.

It is also the story of how Texas, which was once part of Mexico, became an independent nation. And because the independent Republic of Texas, with its Lone Star flag, became later a state in the United States, the story of the Alamo is one of the great American stories and belongs to all of us. To appreciate this story, we have to know a little about what had happened in the wild country of Texas before the time of the Alamo, and what the people were like who came into that wild country.

In 1803 the United States was a great deal smaller than it is now. Florida and the Southwest, from Texas to California, belonged to Spain. All the rest of the land west of the Mississippi River was held by France, which had gotten it earlier from Spain. In 1803 Napoleon, who ruled France, needed money for his wars; so he sold to Thomas Jefferson, as President of the United States, all the French territory. This included the present state of Louisiana and the main part of the western and northwestern country to the Rocky Mountains. The whole territory went under the name of Louisiana.

Spanish territory—Spanish Texas—now lay on our western border. It was a wild country, for though the Spaniards had held the region for about three hundred years, they had not been able to settle it. They had, of course, tried. They had sent in missionaries— friars of the order of St. Francis—to convert the Indians to Christianity. The friars would build missions. There would be a barracks at a mission—a *presidio,* they called it in Spanish—for soldiers to protect the friars. The hope was that the Indians would get converted and consent to settle down as farmers and workmen around the mission. Then white settlers would come in and towns would grow up. This plan had worked very well in settling Mexico. But it did not work at all in Texas.

For one thing, the Texas country was separated from Mexico proper by hundreds of miles of desert and mountain. For a second thing, most of the Texas Indians were very tough Indians. (The Karankawas on the Gulf Coast were enthusiastic cannibals, and the Comanches and Apaches were great horsemen and fighters. The Apaches even went so far as to invite the Spanish to come in and found a mission; then, when the Spanish had done so, the Apaches looted it and killed the occupants.) For a third thing, those tribes that did let themselves be converted were a worthless lot. At the *presidio* of San Antonio, at Bexar where the Alamo stood, a number of Indians did settle, but even the missionaries agreed that they were stupid and filthy.

In spite of all these difficulties some sort of settlement was finally made in Texas. Bexar was the biggest and most important place, the capital of the province of Texas, and the center of our story. The Spanish government had made a special effort to settle Bexar. They had brought in some families from the Canary Islands and had even forcibly imported immigrants from Mexico. But many of these people quickly lost their civilized qualities and their ambition, and weren't much better than the ragtag and bobtail of garrison soldiers or the converted Indians.

Bexar was about what you might expect from such settlers—a few decent buildings where the few more intelligent and decent citizens lived a civilized life, and a huddle of shacks and huts. The most impressive of the buildings was what we know as the Alamo. Then it was known as the Mission of San Antonio de Valero. It consisted of a stone building, a chapel, rooms for the friars, workrooms for Indian women, a storeroom, an inner court, and a walled plaza with the adobe huts of converted Indians.

By 1793 the Mission Valero, as it was called for short, had ceased to be a religious establishment. After nearly a century of missionary work, there were only forty or so converts, and they weren't a kind to be proud of. The mission itself was in bad repair, the walls beginning to crumble and debris to collect in corners. The friars had failed and gone away, and the

6

wild, unconverted horse Indians ranged over the Texas country, even to the outskirts of Bexar.

In Bexar there were now fewer than 2,000 inhabitants, and only a few hundred of these were listed as Spanish, the rest being Indian or of mixed blood. As for the rest of Texas, if we don't count the wild Indians and the small garrisons of troops, there were only about 1,000 people. This was the way things stood when, in 1803, the Louisiana Purchase brought the United States to the border of Spanish Texas.

How did the Mission Valero get the name of Alamo?

The word *alamo* in Spanish means cottonwood tree —a kind of poplar. According to the report handed down in the neighborhood of San Antonio, the grounds around the old Mission Valero once had a grove of cottonwoods along the ditch that supplied the water, and so after the place ceased to be a mission, it gradually took on the name Alamo.

There is another explanation of the name. In 1802 the Spanish government decided to send some reinforcements of troops to Bexar for protection against Indian raids. The troops chosen were a seasoned out-

The friars had failed and gone away.

fit called the Flying Company of San Carlos de Parras, which had been stationed at a place in North Mexico called the Pueblo de San Jose y Santiago del Alamo. The troops had been accustomed to call that place the Alamo.

When they reached Bexar, they found that the old barracks had gone to ruin. So the commander drove out the few Indians and half-breeds that remained in the Mission Valero and settled his troops there. The troops, perhaps out of homesickness for the old quar-

Wild Indians ranged over the Texas country.

ters, called the new station after the old one—the Alamo.

It is fitting that the soldiers of a crack Spanish frontier company—tough Indian fighters—should have given the old mission the name it bears for its military history. For that military history is a bloody one. There was more than one siege and battle of the Alamo, and we shall have to deal with the earlier, less famous occasions for bloodletting before we come to the morning that makes the name immortal.

2

Why the Spaniards
Were Afraid

THE SPANISH GOVERNMENT WASN'T TOO HAPPY TO HAVE the United States on the frontier of Texas. The frontier itself was a possible cause of trouble. It was not clear exactly what Napoleon had sold to Jefferson and whether or not the purchase included Texas. A good many Americans were of the opinion that they had bought Texas from Napoleon. To prevent clashes between Americans and Spaniards a kind of no man's land had been established, but this became a haven for outlaws and land grabbers who waited for any excuse to cross the border.

There was another cause of trouble besides the disagreement about the border line. The Spanish could not help but contrast their own failure to settle Texas with the splendid success of the American expansion westward. The Spaniards knew what the American frontiersman was like, and how he moved into new land like water running downhill. In one way, their worry was not so much about the policy of the United States government toward Texas and the line. It was the worry that the United States, even if it wanted to respect the Texas border, would not be able to restrain the movement of the frontiersmen toward new, unoccupied land.

It has been said that those frontiersmen had no cowards or weaklings among them, for the cowards had never started and the weaklings never got there. This is not true, of course. But they were men brought up to hardship and danger, with pride in their manhood, and there were enough of them who were not cowards or weaklings to give the Spanish government some cause for worry.

It was not just the frontiersman's toughness that the Spanish worried about. The Spanish themselves were tough. They had faced terrific hardship and had conquered a continent. But the American frontiersman had something besides his toughness. He was an individualist. He might pick up his long rifle, whistle to the bear dogs, and head off into the wilderness, followed by his wife and children, who rode on a couple of ponies with a few pots and pans. He was "tarnation fool and consarn idiot enough just to traipse out a little farther, and durn them Indians."

Of course, he might get scalped. But if he did get scalped, there might well be a couple of dead Indians somewhere with the little lead pellet of the long rifle deep in heart or brain. And the next week, or the next year, there would probably be another settler there just like him, and soon there would be another cabin and corn patch among the stumps of trees that had been burned to make a place for scratch farming. There would be a hominy mill made out of a scooped-out stump, and a heavy wood chunk for bruising the grain would hang on a thong from a sapling. A bearskin would be stretched on one wall of the cabin. A path, already worn bare, would lead down to a clear spring. There would be, just inside the door, a new cradle hollowed out of a length of

12

tulip log, and a fiddle hung over the fireplace where the evening pot bubbled.

The Spanish feared the independence of this kind of man, who would get up and go somewhere without waiting for anybody's say-so. And they feared the kind of democracy which these men practiced. The frontiersmen couldn't get it out of their heads that people ought to elect their own government and that government existed for the good of the people. Many frontiersmen and other Americans went to Texas with the honest intention of becoming good Mexican citizens. But they were ripe for trouble when the Mexican government began to change from what they thought a government ought to be.

The notion of democratic government which the honest American settler brought to Texas wasn't the only thing to make the pot of trouble boil. Besides the honest settlers, there were other Americans with an eye on Texas. These were the adventurers.

The small fry among these adventurers might be nothing but border toughs—part-time highwaymen of the sort who infested the trails and traces of the Mississippi Valley or former river pirates who had decided to try dry land. Then, too, there were the smugglers. Spain did not allow trade over the Texas border, and so the illegal business was very appealing to professional smugglers and even to legitimate merchants who had a little money to invest. Nor was that all. The plains of Texas were full of wild horses, any man's for the taking—if he managed to keep his scalp. So there were the mustang raids.

The big fry, however, were not out to smuggle merchandise or run mustangs over the border. They had big ideas. They were out to build nations, or steal empires. They were men like Aaron Burr, who was arrested and tried for attempting to seize the Mississippi Valley for an empire of his own. Or General Wilkinson, who had the notion of grabbing Louisiana and Texas. Or the famous highwayman Murrell, who built up a far-flung secret organization and dreamed of an empire of outlaws. Or the even more famous pirate Jean Lafitte.

But by the time of the Louisiana Purchase there was more for the Spanish government to worry about than American adventurers. The people who lived in Mexico—some of pure Spanish blood, some of mixed Indian and Spanish, and some of pure Indian blood

—had become restless under Spanish rule. Rebellions began. It was to be years before Mexico gained her independence from Spain, but meanwhile the fighting in Mexico gave new excuse for Americans to come in.

Some of the Americans came with the notion that they were helping the cause of liberty by fighting in a war like their own Revolution. Some came because the war gave opportunity for daring and cunning men to become rich and powerful. And some came with a mixture of reasons.

3

First Blood at the Alamo

WE HAVE ALREADY MENTIONED THAT BETWEEN TEXAS
and the United States there was a kind of no man's
land which had become a home for outlaws and desperadoes. The situation grew so bad that American
troops went in to break up the bands. The American
commander was a young lieutenant named Magee.
He was apparently a good soldier, for he managed
to break up the outlaw gangs and scatter them. But
he did more along the border than catch or kill outlaws.

When Magee learned about the war then going on in Mexico—a war that had already come into the Texas territory—the temptation to get into it was too much for him. He was an ambitious young man. Killing outlaws on a lieutenant's pay was all right, but across the Sabine River was wealth and glory for a man who understood war. So Lieutenant Magee resigned from the United States Army and raised a little army of his own. It was a mixed lot of volunteers, including lovers of liberty and unattached Indians as well as some of the bandits whom Magee had just knocked out of employment.

Magee took his army into Texas. There he joined a Mexican named Gutierrez who had been fighting the Spanish. Magee died early in the campaign, but his army knocked all the Spanish forces out of Texas, including even the garrison of the Alamo, at Bexar.

Thus Texas, in 1813, became an independent state, free from Spain. But success ruined the new state. The army had been much swollen by new recruits from across the American border and by Mexicans who had new hope for independence or profit. As long as there was danger some kind of unity was maintained, but as soon as Bexar was taken, things began to come apart at the seams. For one thing, the Americans didn't understand Mexican rules of war and had promised good treatment to the Spanish who surrendered. Therefore, a good many of the Americans were disgusted when the rebels led by Gutierrez sim-

The Alamo

ply butchered the prisoners as systematically and calmly as they might have butchered cattle in a slaughter pen.

As a result, the first battle of the Alamo ended as the last one was to end—with a butchery. The first butchery was committed by those fighting for the cause of freedom, and the last by those fighting against the cause of freedom. There were to be other butcheries in between.

Revenge for the first massacre at the Alamo was not long in coming. A certain General Arredondo led an army into Texas to restore Spanish rule. Arredondo was an experienced soldier with good Spanish training, and the force against him was now more disorganized than ever. After the butchery of the prisoners some of the Americans had left. To make matters worse, the Mexicans hadn't been able to get along too well among themselves, and Gutierrez had been replaced by another Mexican.

As Arredondo approached with his well-organized force and his reputation for winning victories, the rebels could organize no clear plan. Some of the Mexicans refused to fight. A Mexican who refused to fight could simply disappear and feel perfectly safe. He belonged there in the Texas country and wasn't easily identifiable. But with an American it was different. He was a long way from home, and he was a marked man. If he didn't fight and didn't win, there was not a very good chance of his ever getting back home from Texas. If, however, he did fight and win, Texas might make a very comfortable home indeed. It would be a rich country someday.

So the Americans fought.

They fought Arredondo, and they almost won. Man for man, they were fighters, and they knew the value of the cool aim down the long barrel of the frontiersman's rifle. Furthermore, they were not outnumbered. But they were outgeneraled and outguessed and outsmarted. Arredondo drew them into an ambush, into a deadly cross fire in a gorge. Taken by surprise, caught under the muzzles of the hidden muskets and cannon up the slopes, they yet managed to hold on for four hours. Then, when their ammunition was about gone, the survivors fought their way out of the gorge. Of the 850 men who had gone in, only 93 ever got back to the Sabine River.

Some were hunted down and killed on the spot, and some were captured. In two days 112 prisoners were shot—the survivors of the battle of Medina. Bexar, a few miles away, fell immediately, giving 250 more prisoners to Arredondo. Almost all the Americans among these, plus a number of Mexicans, were executed, too.

Arredondo had some excuse for the wholesale

executions. With regard to the Mexican victims, it could be said that he was fighting rebels against a lawful government, and that death is the ordinary

The Americans managed to hold on for four hours.

punishment for rebels and traitors. As for the Americans, Arredondo saw them simply as outlaws who had broken over the frontier and joined up with the rebels.

The bad luck at Medina didn't stop other adventurers with the gambling spirit and a taste for high stakes. Jean Lafitte, the famous pirate, came to Mexico, claiming to defend liberty and independence. He seized Galveston Bay and called himself the Governor of Galveston.

Galveston didn't, however, become the cradle of Mexican independence. It became, instead, the wickedest city in the whole Gulf. Cutthroats, desperadoes, and evil men and women of all kinds gathered here and accepted the rule of Lafitte. It was a tribute to his force of character that he was able to control the place. He built himself a palace at Campeachy, and made himself comfortable with splendid furniture and silver and china, all of it the profit of his piracy. For his piracy was thriving now. As the defender of Mexican independence, he raided the Spanish shipping with a clear conscience and some help from Mexican patriots. He was wise enough to stick to the sea and not carry his successes inland where he might meet somebody like Arredondo.

All the time that Lafitte was taking Spanish ships and acting as the self-declared enemy of Spain he was, in fact, in the pay of the Spanish government as a kind of spy. In his headquarters at Campeachy, he had contact with all sorts of shady characters and heard all the gossip and rumor about desperate projects and adventures in the making. The Spanish realized that one of their best sources of information about plots against their power might be at Galveston. So they paid Lafitte for news. Why not? they reasoned. A pirate's news might be as good as anybody else's news.

On one occasion at least, this opinion proved to be correct. A Louisiana doctor named Long planned to collect a private army and invade Texas. He didn't, however, promise liberty and independence. Instead, he quite frankly said that he was going to make Texas a state in the United States. Like Thomas Jefferson and a good many other Americans, Dr. Long believed that Napoleon had sold Texas to the United States.

Whether or not Dr. Long was right about the legal ownership of Texas, he was wrong to approach Lafitte. He had thought that he and Lafitte might work together, with Lafitte at sea and Long himself on land. Lafitte entertained Dr. Long at his palace in Campeachy and agreed to the arrangement. Then,

Lafitte entertained Dr. Long at his palace.

of course, he sold the secret to the Spanish, and Dr. Long's expedition failed. Later, Long made another effort, and this time got caught. In the end, he was shot.

Dr. Long's project has one connection with the last Battle of the Alamo. Among the volunteers whom he picked up at Campeachy was Jim Bowie, famous for his knife. We shall meet him again at the Alamo.

By 1821, the Spanish had at last been thrown out of Mexico. Mexico was an independent country, a republic with a constitution much like that of the United States. Texas, however, was not a separate state in the United States of Mexico. It had been joined to the state of Coahuila. But the Texans had been promised that as soon as the population should increase enough, Texas would be organized as a separate state in the Mexican nation, with its own legislature and law courts.

Now that Spain was out of the picture, American adventurers could no longer have the excuse of fighting for Mexican independence. American politicians hoped that a peaceful settlement of the Texas boundary could be reached and that Mexico would sell off part, or all, of Texas.

But nothing was really settled. The open land of Texas was still beckoning the frontiersmen across the border. Opportunity for wealth and power was still in the dreams of adventurers. The Spaniards were gone, but the Mexicans remembered with resentment and fear those raids into Texas from the United

States. Can we blame them if they looked upon even honest attempts to buy Texas as part of a dark plot against Mexico?

The Mexicans' continuing failure to settle Texas tended to make them more resentful and suspicious. And as their own failure to set up a firm government and create a strong nation became more marked, their fear of what they called the "North Americans" increased. The Mexicans tried different forms of government. First, there was a republic, then an empire with a proclaimed Emperor, Augustin I, then another republic. And all the time there was plotting and counterplotting, and betraying and counterbetraying, private killing and public war, and a growing despair among responsible citizens.

In all of this disorder, a certain young man was becoming more and more prominent. This young man, already known as a daring soldier, was becoming even better known as a man who could guess just to a hair when to switch sides. And he was on the road to power. His name was Antonio Lopez de Santa Anna, but he is known to history as Santa Anna. He thought of himself as the "Napoleon of the West." He even called himself that, until the road to power led him to the Alamo.

Santa Anna was born in 1794, near Veracruz, in Jalapa, a place whose name means "Water on the Sands." It was a rich and beautiful place, several thousand feet above the Gulf, with a perfect climate and flowers the year round against a background of snowy mountains. The father of Santa Anna, who came from a well-known Spanish family, was a prosperous businessman, a dealer in mortgages. It was only natural that he should want his son to go into business, too. When the boy proved idle and quarrelsome in school, the father found him a job with a prominent merchant in Veracruz. But the boy didn't do any better at business than he had done at school. As he said about himself years later, he wasn't born to be a "counter jumper," as clerks in stores used to be impolitely called.

The upshot was that by social and political influence and by lying about the boy's age, the father got him the place of a cadet in a fine regiment at Veracruz. Santa Anna, just seventeen, had found his career. Within a year, he had the chance to prove that he was made for the military life and the life was made for him.

He was sent north to the Indian frontier. There he saw Indian fighting of the bloody and ruthless sort, and got himself wounded by an arrow and noticed for bravery in action. He was promoted to lieutenant. He had the luck to find a chance to fight not only Indians but also the rebels who were trying to make Mexico independent of Spain. Luckiest of all, he was in the command of Arredondo and could learn from him.

Santa Anna was at the Battle of Medina when the American force was destroyed. Here he was noticed again for bravery, and got a decoration. He saw the occupation of Bexar after the Battle of Medina, and he witnessed the general brutality practiced there and the execution of rebels. Then he participated in more fighting against scattered forces of rebels. By this time he was a captain, with a reputation for leadership in ruthless action.

The young Santa Anna came out of Texas already marked for greatness. He had been lucky in everything—with just one exception. He had had the bad luck to get certain false notions in his head. The first false notion was that absolute ruthlessness was a sure way to terrify an enemy. The second false notion was that regular Mexican troops could easily defeat a rabble of American adventurers.

He had those notions firmly in his head, and they stayed there.

4

Stephen Austin Was an Honest Man

THE METHOD OF SUPPRESSING REBELS WHICH ARREDONDO had used in Texas was not very helpful in settling a country. He believed that it was better to execute three possibly innocent persons than to take the chance of letting one guilty person escape. Consequently population was now on the decline, business was at a standstill, and the Indians were more aggressive than ever. Matters did not improve much when Mexico won her independence from Spain.

The Spaniards had pinned their hope of settling

Texas on a system which they had sometimes used in Louisiana. The idea was to make a large land grant to an American who would then bring in decent and qualified settlers. The man who got the grant—the manager, or *empresario,* as the Spanish called him—had to fulfill several requirements. He had to become a regular citizen of his adopted country. He had to become a Catholic. He had to guarantee the citizenship and religion of his settlers. He had to maintain loyalty, industry, and good order. If he failed in any of these requirements, his grant would be forfeited.

The hope was to set up in Texas a series of such grants to stand as a wall between the Indians and the rest of Texas. The Americans, as the Spanish correctly guessed, would seriously try to farm the land and, once the land was laid out in farms, the horse Indians would be crowded away. The plow would do what Spanish friars and garrisons had failed to do. And if any scalps got lost in the process they would be American and not Spanish scalps.

The first man to try to become an *empresario* was Stephen Austin. Besides being a man of patience and determination, he was a man of honesty and sincerity.

Stephen Austin

It could never be said that he was an adventurer, a mere fortune seeker. The future of Texas, the dream of a new land opening up and prospering, was his very breath of life. "The greatest consolation I ever expect to derive from my labors in the wilderness of this province," he declared to his first settlers, "will arise from the conviction that I have benefited many of my fellow beings, and laid the foundation for the settlement of one of the finest countries in the world." From a man like Austin, these were not empty words. When he took out Mexican citizenship, he did it in good faith. "From the day of my arrival on Mexican soil," he said, "I bade an everlasting farewell to my native country and adopted this, and in doing so I determined to fulfill rigidly all the duties and obligations of a Mexican citizen."

In 1824, only two years after receiving his grant, Austin had the chance to prove his sincerity as a Mexican citizen. Up at Nacogdoches, a settlement near the American frontier, an *empresario* named Edwards held a grant like Austin's. Lawsuits and other friction had developed there about land claims, and some of the new settlers felt that the local courts ruled unfairly against them when the opposing claimant was a Mexican. The *empresario* and his brother did not have the patience and tact of Austin. Before long they had so angered the Mexican government that it ordered the Edwards brothers out of Texas and canceled their grant.

But the Edwards brothers had no intention of leaving Texas. They were far more like Burr and Magee and Long than like Austin. They played for high stakes. They now declared that they were the Republic of Fredonia. They wrote a declaration of independence; they got themselves a flag; they organized what they called an army; they made a treaty with the Cherokees, to whom they looked for military help; and they ousted the Spanish garrison from Nacogdoches. Then they waited for the other Americans in Texas to join them.

Nobody joined them. Austin got the government to agree to forgive the Fredonians and investigate their complaints. He sent some of his leading citizens to appeal to the Edwards, but these citizens accomplished nothing. In fact, when they got back they reported that many of the rebels at Fredonia were "vagabonds and fugitives from justice who have fled from the United States of the North."

This was enough for Austin. He called on his settlers to behave like good, loyal Mexican citizens and put down the revolt of the Fredonians. "To arms, then, my friends and fellow citizens," he commanded, "and hasten to the standard of our country." And when the Mexican troops passed by on the way to Fredonia, the Austin settlers, rifles in hand, joined them on the march.

There was, however, to be no fighting. Even in their own territory the Edwards did not have full support. So when the Mexican troops approached Nacogdoches, the *empresario* and his brother skipped over the border, back to Louisiana.

Though Fredonia ceased to exist when the Edwards brothers fled, it lived on in the imagination and fears of the Mexicans. There was always the danger of another Fredonia. The American settlers were prospering, the plains were coming under the plow, the Indians were being crowded back, population was growing, good times seemed ahead for everybody. All the good things the Mexican government had hoped for from the *empresario* system were coming to pass. But, unfortunately, the more the settlers increased and prospered, the more the Mexicans feared another Fredonia, a Fredonia that would succeed. The Mexican government couldn't seem to remember that Americans had picked up their rifles and marched side by side with Mexican troops to suppress the revolt of Fredonia.

As a result of its fears and suspicions, the Mexican government attempted to bind Texas closer to Mexico by a series of nagging restrictions. During the period between 1824 and 1830, when the new prosperity was coming to Texas, customs duties were kept high or made higher. Consequently, little business could be transacted. Troops, and not always well-disciplined troops, were quartered here and there. Military rule could at any time overturn the ordinary courts.

In addition to the restrictions, the Texans had other complaints. The fact that Texas was not a state meant that it had no high court of its own and the Texans had to go 500 miles to the capital of the state of Coahuila to try a case. They also had little representation in the legislature of Coahuila. But they could cling to the promise in the Mexican Constitution of 1824, which stated that when enough population came to Texas it would be organized as a separate state in the Union of Mexico.

Meanwhile, the United States, sometimes in a very stupid way, had been trying to buy Texas from Mexico. Alarmed by this and by the fact that the Americans in Texas now outnumbered the Mexican Texans almost four to one, the Mexican government passed a law that cut off immigration from the United States. Even Austin protested against this. If immigrants couldn't come, he pointed out, it would take a century to fill the country and business would be at a standstill. Better condemn Texas to the wilderness and the Indians at once and be done with it, he said.

Austin and the American settlers were not the only ones who felt this way. Most Texans of pure Mexican blood saw that to cut off immigration meant to cut off prosperity. And they saw, too, that the anti-immigration law cut off only the better class of settlers. It didn't stop the reckless fellows and desperadoes with no responsibilities or families, the men who were adventurers and sometimes criminals.

Texas was getting ready for trouble, but the first rebellion of the Texans was, strangely enough, against an American. This American was John Davis Bradburn, a Kentuckian by birth. He had become an officer in the Mexican army, and was now in command of a fort called Anahuac on Galveston Bay. He had come with orders to be as tactful as possible in dealing with the Texans. But he was not that kind of a man. He wanted to strike terror, and his soldiers lorded it over the citizens of the region.

Bradburn was, in fact, in a difficult position. The smuggling which he had been ordered to suppress was increasing every day. It didn't even pretend to be secret. Because of the high customs duties on imported goods and the other restrictions of the Mexican government, the citizens supported the smugglers. Only from the smugglers could they get the supplies and tools and ordinary merchandise they needed. They didn't hesitate to lay hands on a customs official or get out their guns to protect a smuggler craft as it made out of the harbor.

5

A Young Fellow Who Didn't Mind Trouble

THERE HAPPENED TO BE IN THE NEIGHBORHOOD A YOUNG fellow who didn't mind trouble. This young man was William Barret Travis. His friends called him Buck Travis. Travis was not one of the border desperadoes or toughs who kept drifting into Texas. If he was an adventurer, he was of another stamp, a man of education and training who was not afraid of a hard life and could carry himself with hard men.

Travis had been born in South Carolina, and had gone to school there. It was said that he had been expelled before graduation for taking part in a student rebellion. If that is true, we see there the first early step on the way toward the Alamo. But the way was to have many windings. Travis turned up next in Alabama. There he studied and practiced law, made money, got married, had a son and daughter. The prospects seemed bright for the young lawyer, for Alabama was then coming out of its frontier stage into a solid prosperity.

But something went wrong. Travis and his wife quarreled. He took the son, left the daughter with his wife, got a divorce, and went to Texas to start life over again. Yes, Texas was the place to begin over.

Travis, by good or bad luck, settled near Anahuac, where Colonel John Bradburn represented the Mexican law. We must realize that Buck Travis didn't have much respect for Mexican law to begin with. In fact, his very presence in Texas was a violation of Mexican law, for he had come in after the law forbidding immigration from the United States. He soon had even less respect for the Mexican law as vested in the person of Colonel Bradburn. And so, according to one account, he tried to take the law into his own hands.

This occasion was, if the story is true, the real spark

William Barret Travis

of the Texas Revolution. According to the account, five Mexican soldiers from Bradburn's garrison had insulted and mistreated the wife of a settler. Bradburn would do nothing about it. Travis collected a dozen or so men, captured a Mexican soldier—according to some accounts not one of the offenders—and under the very shadow of Anahuac set about the old frontier punishment of tar and feathers.

But Bradburn and his troops turned up and cap-

41

tured Travis and his friends. Word got out that Bradburn would not turn his prisoners over to a civil court but would send them back to Mexico for trial. And now things began to happen. For no matter how irresponsible Travis and his friends had been, some very responsible and respectable men took up the cause. Runners went out to summon armed men, and armed men gathered.

The first group to assemble had a rendezvous on the Trinity River near a town called Liberty. They elected a captain and started toward the fort, not even waiting for reinforcements from more distant settlements. As it happened, they were in luck. They surprised a detachment of Bradburn's cavalry, seized the troops, and tied them up. Now they, too, had some prisoners.

Meanwhile, alarmed by the prospect of real disorder, some Mexican officers and officials and some Americans tried to patch things up. Bradburn agreed to exchange the prisoners. The Americans kept their part of the agreement and turned the Mexican cavalrymen loose. But Bradburn kept his prisoners.

The rebels, or whatever we should call them, had now gone too far to retract. Now that Bradburn's trick had showed his true attitude, they had to finish Bradburn or he would finish them. They had to take the fort.

To take a fort they needed cannon, and the nearest cannon, except for those in Bradburn's hands, were across the country at Brazoria. So a solid detachment set out for Brazoria to pick up two brass cannon. Once the rebels had the cannon, they decided to return by sea. It would be easier than dragging the metal overland in June weather.

But to go by sea, they had to pass a Mexican fort at Velasco. That fort was in command of a certain Colonel Ugartechea who had indicated earlier that he thought Bradburn had exceeded his authority. Because of this the Americans thought that he would sympathize with them, and so they asked for permission to pass. But even if the Colonel did sympathize with the Americans, he couldn't wink at preparations for a full-scale rebellion. He refused passage past the fort.

The Colonel promptly had a full-scale battle on his hands. The schooner bringing the cannon downriver from Brazoria came within range and opened fire, and the rebel riflemen surrounded the fort. Except for the two cannon on the schooner, the Mexicans had the artillery. But a man has to put his hand to a cannon to fire it, and some of the riflemen could hit a hand about as far as they could see it. After a while there simply weren't enough unwounded hands in the fort to man the artillery. In addition, there were some dead soldiers. So the fort surrendered.

The rebels now had the cannon to make a try for the fort at Anahuac. But they didn't have to make the try. The senior officer for East Texas, Colonel Jose de las Piedras, commandant of the Mexican forces at Nacogdoches, had heard of the trouble and had marched to investigate. Near Anahuac he found himself a prisoner of the rebels. Or, if prisoner is too strong a word, he found himself respectfully surrounded by them. Since he was aware of Bradburn's abuse of authority, he promised to remove Bradburn from command, to end the military rule established by Bradburn, to pay for property confiscated by Bradburn, and to release Bradburn's prisoners. Colonel de las Piedras was as good as his word. Bradburn was soon on his way to Louisiana and William Barret Travis was free.

Now, through the strange confusion of revolution

and counter-revolution in Mexico and the rebellion in Texas, Travis and Santa Anna were on the same side. Not that Santa Anna, in far-off Mexico, would have heard of the young lawyer who had got himself in trouble at Anahuac. But Travis, like everybody else in Texas, would have heard of Santa Anna. For Santa Anna was now famous, and, at the age of thirty-six, he was probably the strongest man in Mexico. He was regarded by many good and respectable people in Mexico as the only man who could establish a stable government. Already a revolution was under way, and armies were in the field in his name. Thus both Santa Anna and Travis, with his Texans, were fighting the established Mexican government.

Not all of Texas, however, was ready for Santa Anna's leadership. By the time Travis was released, many Texans, including a great number of Americans who had taken out Mexican citizenship, were ready to declare their loyalty to the established government —the government which Santa Anna was trying to overthrow. In other words, in spite of all that had happened—high customs duties and laws against immigration and the high-handed behavior of troops— the main body of opinion was for loyalty even to a bad Mexican government and for peace at any price.

But things were moving fast. Within a matter of weeks, Mexican troops friendly to Santa Anna had come into Texas. And by this time Stephen Austin, still the most influential man in Texas, had come to place his only hope for order and decency on Santa Anna. The Texas Americans now swung to the cause of Santa Anna. But they insisted, in a resolution sent to the Mexican commander, that they were loyal Mexicans: "We are Mexicans by adoption, we are the same in heart and will remain so."

The Mexican commander was, it appears, well satisfied with their loyalty. There was a great banquet, with toasts drunk to Santa Anna and the Republic of Mexico.

But even while the toasts were being drunk something was happening down in Mexico to make the situation uneasy. The agent of the United States government in Mexico had been trying to buy Texas, and his methods had been neither wise nor decent. His behavior had been such that it was generally believed he had had a hand in the uprising in Texas. He seemed to think that mixing in an underhanded way in Mexican politics and trying to bribe Mexican officials was acceptable conduct for a diplomat. His conduct greatly increased the Mexican distrust of the United States. That distrust, in fact, grew so great that when, in 1832, the Senate ratified a treaty renouncing all claim to Texas, the ratification was taken as only another American trick.

It was true that Americans were interested in Texas. They were keenly interested in it. Many wanted to go there, and even to become Mexican citizens. Many others wanted the United States to buy it, to make it a part of the country. But to want to go there, or to want to buy Texas, was not exactly the same thing as to want to take it by force of arms. Even Andrew Jackson, who was now President and who was famous for direct action, didn't want to take it by force of arms. But he did want it, and when his old friend Sam Houston went to Texas in August, 1832, to investigate the situation, Jackson awaited his letters with great interest.

6

Sam Houston Gets a Razor

THE HOUSTONS, A FAMILY OF SCOTCH DESCENT, HAD BEEN
in America over a hundred years when Sam went to
Texas. They had had a fine plantation in Virginia,
and Sam's father had been an officer in the Revolution and an important man. However, when he died
he was poor. The plantation had already been sold
for debt, and all the widow had was some wild land
in Tennessee. So she loaded up her nine children and
household gear on two wagons and set out for the wilderness. In 1807, Blount County, Tennessee, was little
more than a wilderness.

It was a wilderness that exactly suited young Sam Houston. He had never liked school. The woods had always been his favorite place, and now with the Cherokee nation only a few miles from his cabin door, a whole life of wild lore was open to him. When he was a little older he was sent out to work in a store, but "counter jumping" suited him as little as it did the young Santa Anna in far-off Veracruz, about this same time. So Sam ran away to the Indians. He lived with them, learning their woodcraft, absorbing their harmony with nature, coming to respect and admire them. If he had not come into the wilderness when he was young and impressionable, just under thirteen, how different his life might have been.

He learned the life of the frontier, the loneliness, the self-reliance. But we must not think of him as a simple hunter and woodsman, a white man gone half Indian. Even if young Houston did not like school, he loved books and read everything he could lay hands on. He was the sort of boy who didn't need school. His head was full of the ambition to read Greek, to read Homer's poem about the Greek and Trojan heroes and the fall of Troy. In the wilderness he carried a copy of Pope's translation of the *Iliad* in his pocket. We are apt to think of the boy squatting in a thicket, watching by the hour the grazing deer or a bear busy at his bee tree. But we must also think of him lying by a stream, where it plunges over the gray limestone falls, and quoting at the top of his voice, against the racket of the tumbling water, the poetry of the most heroic of all wars. For by the Indian campfire, the tall gangly boy with a hunting shirt of red calico and brown hair in a queue down his back had crouched over his book and memorized Homer.

The way to his heroism, his greatness, began early. By the time he was twenty-one, the War of 1812 with England was on, and Houston became a soldier—first as a private, then as an ensign. His fighting was not against the British, but against Indians. He didn't fight his friends the Cherokees, but the Creeks, down in Alabama. He was with the army of Andrew Jackson at the Battle of Horseshoe Bend. In the thick of the fighting he got an arrow deep in his left thigh. Under the threat of a lifted sword Houston forced a friend to jerk the barb from his flesh. Then, while a surgeon tried to stop the gush of blood, the meeting took place that was to shape Houston's whole life.

General Jackson—the great Jackson, not yet the victor of New Orleans and the President, but already great—rode up. He ordered the boy to the rear. When Houston protested, Jackson made the order absolute and turned away. He was not accustomed to having his orders disobeyed.

A few minutes later, in a moment of crisis, Jackson called for volunteers to storm a Creek position strongly situated up a ravine. It was a desperate effort. The battle might hinge on it. But nobody responded. Then, suddenly, Houston, whose refusal to go to the rear had as yet passed unnoticed by Jackson, shouted to his own little detachment, and plunged forward toward the Indian position. At the very entrance of the ravine he was hit, and fell.

He was alone. Not a man had followed him. But once he was down, the attack swung forward, and the battle was won.

Houston was down with two wounds in his right shoulder, and the bone of the upper arm was badly shattered. The wound never healed properly, but it made Jackson the firm friend of Houston for life. Though Jackson was not used to being disobeyed, he

The arrow struck deep in his left thigh.

saw that Houston's disobedience had been the result of
a fighting heart, and that was what Jackson loved
most.

Houston recovered enough to get back into uni-
form, with a commission in the regular army; but for
him fighting was over for a long time to come. He became Indian agent to his old friends, the Cherokees.

But his business with them was now a sad one. He had the duty of persuading them to give up their lands and move west. Something of the state of his sympathies and of the Cherokees' trust in him is shown by the fact that, when he went to Washington with the Indians to make the treaty for the removal west, Houston wore Indian costume. The Indians had asked him to wear it.

The whole affair of the Indian removal turned out badly for Houston and he found himself the victim of political intrigue. So he gave up his commission, went to Nashville, Tennessee, and began the study of law. He got his license, and began to practice in a tiny log cabin in the village of Lebanon, just outside of Nashville. He was penniless, but he was brilliant, and he had friends. Among those friends was Jackson, now the victor of New Orleans and a power in national politics. As a friend and young protégé of Jackson, Houston was often at Jackson's great house, the Hermitage. He met the great and powerful men who gathered there and began to get the sense of politics, to understand how power is made and grasped. By 1823, when he was thirty, Houston was a congressman from Tennessee.

Houston was clearly meant for success. He was handsome and vigorous. He had a romantic past, the past of the battlefield and its honorable scars, of the deep forest and the Indian campfire. He fascinated people and drew them to him. He was something of an actor, and instinctively could present his own personality as complex and interesting. And he had a conviction that somewhere, somehow, greatness was waiting for him. How could he be wrong? His protector, Jackson, was surely moving toward the presidency. Houston himself became governor of Tennessee while still very young. He had just married a rich and charming girl, Eliza Allen. He could hope for and expect everything.

Then, all at once, he had nothing.

One day he left home to make the first big speech of the new political campaign for his second term as governor. The speech went well. But when he got back home, his bride was gone. She had fled back to her father's house in the next county. We do not know what lay behind this. No word ever came from the Allen family, and no word from Houston. But there must have been something more than a mere quarrel, some dark and shattering trouble between them. In any case, the effect was shattering on Houston.

He resigned as governor of Tennessee, left all his hopes and ambitions behind him, and fled west. There was only one place for him to flee—to the wilderness, to the Indians, to the recollection of the time when he had been happy.

In the Arkansas Territory, where the Cherokees had been settled, the old chief *Oo-loo-te-ka* put his arms around the fugitive and said: "My son, my son! My people are yours. Rest with us." There was a big feast for Houston, and later he was to say that, when he had laid himself down to sleep that night, he felt "like a weary wanderer returned at last to his father's house."

But this mood of happiness did not last. After all, Sam Houston was not an Indian and he was an intensely ambitious man, probably not too certain of what he wanted out of life, but full of dark energies that had to be used. Now he could not use them. Fishing, hunting, living with nature and in communion with the Indians—that was no longer enough. So Houston took to brooding idleness. Days would pass while he sat in a deep depression. He had fits of aimless violence, brought on by his despair and grief for his ruined marriage and thwarted career. He took to drink and would lie for hours, sometimes a day and a night, in a stupor. The Indians began to call him Big Drunk. There was a chance that he might become what was not too uncommon on the frontier—the white man who, ruined by life, took refuge with the Indians until, sodden with drink and debauchery, he sank beneath their contempt.

It is likely that Houston's own despair was not helped much by the fact that the Indians had fallen on evil days. The land promised them in Arkansas Territory was not up to expectations. Food was short. They were unhappy. And even here they were already feeling the pressure of the white man. But out of his own despair and the despair of the Indians may have come the rebirth of Houston.

Rumors got back to Washington, to the ears of Andrew Jackson, now the President. The rumors were extraordinary and incredible but, with a man like Houston involved, perhaps true. The rumors ran that *Oo-loo-te-ka* was building up a great secret confederacy among the Indians of the West, and that with this force he and Houston planned to conquer Texas, even Mexico, and set up an empire. It was the old dream of Burr, of Wilkinson, of Murrell. This time it might come true.

Jackson was the friend of Houston. He admired and trusted him. Instead of going behind Houston's back, Jackson wrote him a direct letter, asking if the rumors were true. Houston accepted the letter as an act of friendship, knowing that Jackson might have ignored him and relied on government sources of information. He promised Jackson that if he decided to leave what he called his "seclusion," he would consult the President first. And he added, rather vaguely, that he might give aid in "some struggle between usurpation, and the rights of the people." That almost certainly meant Texas.

In December, 1831, the Cherokees sent a delegation to Washington. Houston accompanied the delegation and wore the dress of a chief of one of the "civilized tribes"—buckskin coat with beads and silver trim and a big felt hat with beads, silver, and a white eagle feather. He was a romantic and imposing figure.

In Washington Houston became involved in more than Indian business. A congressman referred to him in a speech as one of Andrew Jackson's "bullies." When the congressman refused Houston's challenge to a duel, Houston sought him out on the street and beat him. There was a long trial before the House of Representatives. Francis Scott Key, who had written "The Star-Spangled Banner," was Houston's lawyer, but it was Houston's own speech that swept the country and made him a hero of Jackson's party. "Though it may be alleged," Houston said in his speech, "that I am a man of broken fortune and blasted reputation, I never can forget that reputation, however limited, is the high boon of heaven. Perhaps the circumstances of adversity, by which I have been crushed, have made me cling to the little remains of it I possess, and to cherish them with greater fondness."

Houston did get fined $500, but the fine was remitted by the President. Houston became a national figure, and went on a mission to Texas.

We do not know that Jackson sent him, but we do know what Houston wanted. Trouble was bound to break out in Texas, and Houston wanted to be there when it happened.

So on December 2, 1832, by the ruins of an old fort on the Texas border, Houston sat on his horse and looked across the Red River into the strange land

Houston sought him out and beat him.

where he was going. A friend was there to tell
him good-bye. They might never meet again. The
friend wanted to give Houston a present, a remem-
brance. All he had available was a fine razor. Houston took it, thanked the friend, then added: "If I

have luck, this razor will some day shave the chin of the president of a republic."

Then he rode his horse into the swollen river, and crossed over. He had left his "seclusion." By Christmas he was down in the Stephen Austin grant. There he had Christmas dinner with Jim Bowie. The participants in the story of the Alamo were gradually coming together.

7

Jim Bowie: The Deadliest
Man Alive

JIM BOWIE, WITH WHOM HOUSTON HAD HIS FIRST CHRIST-
mas dinner in Texas, did not invent the bowie knife.
There are several conflicting accounts of its origin. According to one account, it was invented by one of Jim
Bowie's brothers. According to another, it was invented by a man named Black, a New Jersey man who
had been an apprentice to a silversmith before drifting west.

At the settlement of Washington, in the Arkansas
Territory, Black specialized in knives. He knew how to

work delicate scrolls of silver or gold into the hardest steel. But most important, he developed a new steel, a secret process never seen by any eye but his own. Every knife had his loving care. Every blade had to pass the hickory test. In other words, after being used in whittling for an hour on a block of seasoned hickory it still had to remain sharp enough to shave the hair, dry, off a man's arm. Arkansas was a rough place, a place where such a blade would become famous. And the steel of James Black was known up and down the Mississippi, in Missouri, and in the streets and hotels of New Orleans. It was also known, naturally, in Texas.

Up the trail from Texas, in December, 1830, Jim Bowie came riding. He was already the famous Jim Bowie, a big, handsome, auburn-haired, gray-eyed man, very quiet and courteous in his manner, the hero of a dozen tales of death by the knife blade. He stopped at Black's shop. He could use Black's steel. He had brought a model of his own design, carefully whittled out of soft wood. He would leave the model with Black, and stop for the knife on his way back to Texas.

When Bowie came back, Black had the knife. But

he had another one, too, made from a new design of his own. He thought it would best suit the Jim Bowie of the bloody tales. Jim Bowie looked at the knife. He hefted it, felt its delicate balance. He knew that it was the knife for him. Within a few days it had saved his life in a fight against three bullies who ambushed him on the road.

Bowie, as we have said, was already famous. And now this new kind of knife—a knife good enough for a job of one against three—shared his fame. Other men wanted a knife like Jim Bowie's—a bowie knife.

What was the bowie knife like? It was, of course, a development from the frontiersman's hunting knife. But the hunting knife was a work knife. It was a blade set in a simple haft, about like an ordinary butcher knife. In fact, it was sometimes called a butcher knife.

The bowie, however, was not a work knife. It was heavy and long, up to twenty-odd inches. The blade was single-edged from the haft to the curving-back point, and then double-edged on the reverse of the curve for a few inches. A man doesn't need a reverse edge for cutting meat or strap leather. Nor does he need a pronged guard on a work knife, or a blade with brass tempered into the squared back of the steel. But he does need a guard if he doesn't want another knife to slip to his hand when blades clash in air. And when blades clash, it is useful to have that brass strip into which the opponent's knife edge will nick and be held so it can't slip.

The bowie knife

How did a man use a bowie knife? In a rough-and-tumble "medley" he did the best he could—chop, plunge, or slash. But the real knife fighter, up against another knife fighter, aimed for the body. He held the knife sidewise, the thumb along the blade below the cross guard to brace his blow. He set his left foot well forward and held his head back. Now he was set for a slash to either side or for the up-slash, the stroke to the belly.

This was the knife which Bowie took to the Alamo,

and which Davy Crockett saw there. According to what purports to be an autobiography of Crockett, Bowie saw him gazing at the knife. "Colonel," Bowie said, "you might tickle a fellow's ribs a long time with this little instrument before you'd make him laugh, and many a time I've seen a man puke at the thought of the point touching the pit of his stomach." The purported autobiography is not authentic, but authentic or not, it told the truth about the bowie knife.

The Bowie family, like the Houston family, was Scottish, and had come to America before the Revolutionary War. There is some dispute about the date and place of Jim Bowie's birth. A good argument, however, puts it in 1796, in Logan County, Kentucky, just north of Nashville, Tennessee. In any case, it is certain that the family was in Louisiana when Jim was a small boy. There Jim Bowie, like the young Sam Houston, found his wilderness, a land of dense forests, black-water swamps, winding bayous.

The family prospered with a big plantation, but the wilderness and the wild Cajun boys—descendants of French settlers—were an important part of Jim's life and that of his two brothers. Even in that section, where daring was common, Jim was famous at an early age. He was famous for the sport of riding alligators and the sport of lassoing wild cattle. Violence and adventure were part of his life. He was never to lose a taste for them. And they developed, too, his rugged physique, quickness of eye, incredible coordination in action, and coolness of nerve.

Jim Bowie came early to his strength and his independence. By the time he was seventeen or eighteen, he was in a sawmill business with his brothers, and prospering. But this was too dull. So he and his brothers took some of their profits, fitted out some small boats, and sailed away to Galveston, the stronghold of the "respectable pirate," Jean Lafitte. They intended to buy slaves from Lafitte and run them into the United States. Lafitte took a liking to Jim and ended by giving him almost a monopoly on the business. It was a rough world the Bowies were bred to.

At Galveston Jim Bowie first saw Texas. He saw the coast plains and the tangle of inlets. And once he pursued inland a band of Indians that had snapped up some of his newly purchased slaves. So he saw something of the country beyond the coast. At Lafitte's stronghold he heard wild tales of wealth to be made in Texas, and of the adventure to be had. He even joined up for the expedition of Dr. Long—the expedition that Lafitte betrayed to the Spaniards. That betrayal ended Bowie's interest in Texas. But only for the time being.

He quit his slaving and went into land speculation. A land speculator's life was a wandering one, full of adventure. Bowie was seen everywhere—in the wilderness and in the drawing rooms of New Orleans—dressed either in the rough clothes of the woodsman or the quiet elegance of a prosperous gentleman. Wherever he went he was known. He was known for good fellowship with many kinds of men. He was known for veracity and generosity with money. He was known for a very courteous manner, the quiet air of a gentleman of cultivation. He was "always a gentleman and patriot," as Henry Clay is reported to have called him.

But Bowie was also known for the big knife. His name was often in the papers, and not all the stories were legend. Bowie may have been a quiet fellow, but somehow, when he was frequenting the rough world of the wilderness, he was liable to be in the center of some action, with his gray eyes watchful and his thumb set flat along the side of the heavy blade just under the cross-guard.

In 1829 Jim Bowie was back in Texas. There was opportunity here for a land speculator. But there was something more. Bowie had been drawn to Ursula Verimendi, the beautiful young daughter of a powerful, rich, and aristocratic family of Bexar. It was a love match, the crowning event of the romantic career of Jim Bowie. The bride, by the way, was the goddaughter of Santa Anna. That seemed appropriate, too, for Santa Anna was generally regarded then as the defender of decency and good government.

Jim Bowie settled down. There were no more tales of knife encounters. He was busy with a weaving mill and his land operations. He took out Mexican citizenship. He was wealthy and growing wealthier. There were, very quickly, two babies—a girl and a boy. The world seemed perfect for Jim Bowie.

There was, however, the trouble of the little revolt which Buck Travis sparked over at Anahuac and which wound up as a revolution in favor of Santa Anna. Bowie did get involved in that. It was Bowie

Jim Bowie was known for the big knife.

who, with twenty horsemen, cut off the garrison retreating from Nacogdoches and accepted their surrender. There had not been much of a fight. The
Mexicans were ready to go over to the Santa Anna
party.

It was not long afterward that Bowie had Christmas dinner with Sam Houston.

8

Trouble Means Texas

FOR A WHILE AFTER SANTA ANNA CAME TO POWER, there were high hopes in Texas for peace and a liberal government that would reduce tariffs, establish coastwise trade with Mexico proper, renew immigration, remove military rule, and establish Texas as a separate state in the Mexican republic. There was good evidence that the hopes would be realized. Immigration was again permitted, and it was generally assumed that when a petition was drawn up for separate statehood the request would be granted. Austin himself took the petition to Mexico City. But nothing happened. Santa Anna expressed interest, but would promise no action.

Weeks passed and then, for the first time, the discreet Austin did an indiscreet thing. He wrote a letter in which he said that if the Texans were to go ahead and set up their state—one loyal to Mexico, however —it would probably be accepted. This letter was opened by Mexican officials, who were spying on Austin's correspondence. He was arrested. There was a long legal tangle about the charge on which he might be tried. But meanwhile he was kept in jail, for a time in solitary confinement. Even now his first thought was to maintain peace in Texas. He sent word that nothing should be done on his behalf, that the people should continue their normal life and their loyalty to the government.

Texas did remain quiet, at least for the most part. A war party developed under the leadership of people like the hot-headed Buck Travis, but generally speaking the people remained quiet. They wanted to develop business and farming. Besides, they had faith in Austin.

However, things began to play into the hands of the war party. Santa Anna, who had seemed the hope of men wanting orderly democratic government, began to unmask his true designs. He was destroying the old United States of Mexico and setting himself up as a dictator. When there was opposition to this, he was merciless. But he did finally let Austin out of jail. No doubt he assumed that Austin had learned his lesson and would go back to Texas with the report that resistance was useless.

If Austin had learned a lesson it was not this one. The night he landed on Texas soil he walked the beach all night, weighing a decision. Then, at a dinner given in his honor, he made a speech. "The constitutional rights and security and peace of Texas ought to be maintained," he said. And ten days later, with a Mexican army approaching by sea, he said: "War is our only resource. There is no other remedy but to defend our rights, our country, and ourselves by force of arms."

What were they prepared to fight for? They were prepared to fight for the old Mexican Constitution of 1824, a republican form of government for all Mexico, with Texas only another state in that union. In other words, they were opposing the revolution of Santa Anna, who had set himself up as dictator. A convention assembled to set up a Provisional Government of the Mexican State of Texas, with Henry Smith as governor and Sam Houston as commander in chief. Austin was to go to the United States to seek help.

Meanwhile, the commander of the Alamo had sent a detachment of troops to the town of Gonzales to take possession of a cannon which the Mexican government had given that settlement for protection against Indians. Under the present uneasy conditions, the commander of the Alamo thought it might be better to have the cannon inside his walls rather than outside them. But when his troops got to Gonzales, they found armed Texans under a banner bearing the words: "Come and Take It."

The Mexican troops did not seriously try to take the brass cannon until General Cos, the father-in-law of Santa Anna, arrived with reinforcements. Then a much stronger force went out. But it wasn't strong enough. By this time Texans were pouring into Gonzales. So the Mexicans went back to the Alamo.

The Texans at Gonzales, heartened by their successful brush with Mexican troops, decided to go to the Alamo themselves and knock that garrison out of Texas. It was October of 1835 when they headed for Bexar.

The armed mob that set out for Bexar could scarcely

The Texans' banner read, "Come and Take It."

be called an army at all. There was no military organization to speak of, no very clear idea of where
authority lay, there were no supplies, and no artillery except the little brass cannon which the Mexicans had unsuccessfully tried to carry away. (This
the Texans abandoned on the way.) They picked up
recruits as they went—men riding in from the east,
some Americans adventuring in from home, ready
for trouble. Among the Texas recruits were the famous
scout Deaf Smith and the great Jim Bowie himself, but
not the same Jim Bowie we last saw, happily married
and the father of two children. The wife and children
had died, victims of a cholera epidemic. What had
stabilized Bowie's life was now gone. He was ready
for the most desperate chances.

Lying in a bend of the San Antonio River, swathed
in a fog so dense that the attacking Mexicans could
not be detected until the jingling of their spurs gave
them away, the Texans were surprised by troops
from the Alamo. They stumbled into position and,
when the sun had burned the fog away, they held on
along the river. Bowie was there, going along the line,
saying, "Be cool, boys, be cool. Take your time. Shoot
to hit. Don't waste powder, boys, shoot to hit, boys."

When the Mexicans brought up their brass field-piece, set it up some eighty yards off, and blazed away with grape and canister, the Texans did as they had been told. They shot to hit. Three times their rifles knocked the gun crew off the gun, and three times the Mexican officers managed to rally men to serve it. Then Jim Bowie shouted: "The cannon, boys! Let's take the cannon!"

There was a wild yell, a dash across eighty yards under the fire of the Mexicans, who held on for another moment, and then the cannon was overwhelmed. Ready loaded for the next Mexican hand bold enough to be laid on it, the cannon was wheeled around. This time a Texas hand touched it off, and grape and canister hit the back of the fleeing enemy. The battle of La Concepcion was over.

Bowie had done more than shout for the charge. He had led it.

The Texans were at their best laying a cool eye down the rifle barrel or charging those eighty yards trying to catch up with Jim Bowie. But they were far from their best as an army trying to lay siege to a fort. In the Alamo there were about 800 Mexicans under General Cos. The Texans outnumbered the Mexicans and their numbers were growing daily.

More Texans were coming in, men who had not been able to come before. But also there were the frontiersmen from the United States, men with the powder horn, the long rifle, a pony, slow speech, hands hard as horn, and faces like whit-leather. There were also young men from Louisiana. Some were rough characters from the waterfront of New Orleans, but there were men of education and manner, too, equally drawn to the chance of wealth and adventure.

In the Texas army there was no artillery, and no plan of action. The army lay outside Bexar in idleness. The days passed into November, with fog, rain, wet ground, chill weather. The men huddled about their fires and wondered why they were there, doing nothing. This wasn't the kind of war they had bargained for. They began to walk away, to ride off. It wasn't desertion. They hadn't sworn anything. They were just disgusted.

Among those who remained was a man named Ben Milam, already famous in Texas. He had had enough of this dawdling. One day in early December, when the morale was at bottom, he went into the tent of Burleson, the commander. The other men stood outside staring at the tent. When Milam came out he yelled for attention, then waved his old slouch hat. "Boys," he yelled, "who'll go with old Ben Milam into Bexar?"

They went.

It was, however, slow going. Bit by bit, they penetrated the town, fighting from house to house, trying to stay clear of the streets, which could be swept by cannon fire from the Alamo and fortified plaza. The Texans inched forward, trying for shots at the Mexican troops who held the roofs. Meanwhile, the Mexicans on the roofs developed a decided disinclination to raising their heads to take proper aim.

By the afternoon of the second day, the Texans had fought into the neighborhood of the plaza. By the night of December 8th, they had encouraging news. A captured Mexican officer said that the garrison was hungry and resentful, and that some of the officers had given up hope. In fact, there was a plot for one of Cos's most trusted officers to desert with his men and escape.

Cos had already given orders to draw back all forces from the plaza and assemble in the Alamo for a last stand. But some of his officers had no stomach for this. That very night those officers quietly disappeared with 170 men. To make matters worse for Cos, the cunning scout Deaf Smith put out the rumor to citizens of the town that the deserters had joined the Texans against Santa Anna.

The morning came cloudy and damp. The Texans lying in the houses and on the roofs to the north of the plaza were ready for the day's fight. They hoped that it would be the last. Anyway, they thought they ought to have the town cleared by night, and be ready to knock at the gates of the Alamo. Then, across the plaza, they saw movement in the Mexican lines. The defenders were drawing back, back into the Alamo, leaving their only gun outside, a little four-pounder.

A bit later, across the plaza, coming into range of the rifles, three Mexican officers appeared with a bugler. The officers wore their swords, no other arms. They were alone except for the bugler. The bugler raised his instrument, and blew the call to parley.

The Texans had not had the advantage of a military education. What they knew about war they had had to pick up as they went along. They had not had the chance to pick up the information that this was a call to parley. They didn't figure it out until one of the Mexican officers, impatient at Texan dullness, waved a white handkerchief. That made more sense to the Texans.

Discussion of terms of surrender began. General Cos demanded that he be allowed to march out with flying colors, that the Texans fire a salute to his flag, that he be allowed to take his artillery, ammunition, and stores, that the Texans provision his army to Laredo, and that his parole should end when he crossed the Rio Grande. He wanted so many other things that he seemed to have forgotten who was doing the surrendering.

The Texas commander refreshed his memory. "Powder is as cheap as provisions," he said, "and we still have powder."

Four days later Cos led his army down toward Mexico, and on the Texan terms, with no end date for parole. But there might just as well have been an end date. An oath was no oath to Cos when given to a Texan.

Now the Alamo and, in fact, all of Texas, was in the hands of the Texans. The victory had cost something. Among the dead was Ben Milam, who had put an end to the dawdling.

9

"We Will Rather Die in These Ditches . . ."

THERE WAS GENERAL REJOICING IN TEXAS. BUT THERE was also a general collapse in the conduct of Texan affairs. Things had been bad before the siege operations; with victory, they were even worse. Men wanted to go home for Christmas. If any Mexicans were fool enough to want to come back, they'd knock 'em out again. Men who had signed up for a regular term, sixty days, now left when their time was up. The others, who had walked or ridden in on their own, just went off again. If volunteers hadn't kept on coming from the United States, there would have been no force in the field. As for the volunteers, they were usually very dissatisfied on arrival. They had missed the action and were bored. Besides, the Texas government didn't have any money to pay men.

To make matters worse, the Texas provisional government was split into bitter factions, with Henry Smith on one side and the Council on the other. Neither side was able to enforce its authority. This was particularly bad for the military situation, for despite the victory at the Alamo a big Mexican army was gathering below the Rio Grande under the command of Santa Anna himself, the "Napoleon of the West."

Sam Houston, the commander in chief, realized some of the dangers. He was enough of a soldier to know that most victories require more systematic preparation and dreary drudgery than had been necessary at the battle of La Concepcion and at the Alamo. He was trying to build up a regular army with discipline and an understanding of war over the long pull. But the Texas forces in the field were melting away. Besides, most people held that the volunteers who came down from the United States weren't under Houston's command anyway.

Santa Anna called himself the "Napoleon of the West."

What brought the bad business to a head and invited disaster was the Matamoros expedition. This project was the work of a certain Dr. James Grant. Dr. Grant had been a rich landowner down in the state of Coahuila, a Scot who had come to Mexico and done well. As a strong supporter of the old Mexican system, he had had to flee when Santa Anna became dictator. His estates, of course, were seized. Now he had thrown in his lot with the Texans. He had been an aide to the commander at the attack on Bexar, and had been wounded.

His idea, which turned out to be a tragic one for Texas, was to spark a revolution against Santa Anna down in Mexico itself. Dr. Grant wanted to lead the army, while it was flushed with the victory of Bexar, to the Mexican port town of Matamoros and capture it.

There was some sense to Grant's plan. There was opposition in Mexico to Santa Anna, and an invasion would encourage it. As for Matamoros itself, to seize the place would deprive Santa Anna of a valuable base for operations against Texas. Furthermore, Matamoros was a rich port, and—let us not forget this fact—some of the Texas army did not think badly of the prospect of some pillage. It is unpleasant to remember that the conduct of the army at Bexar was not always decent. In fact, as one Texan who was there was to say later, the practices of the army were "a shame and a disgrace to the American name."

There was, on the other hand, a strong military argument against the expedition. To send the expedition, the Texans would have to divide their army. Would it not be better to concentrate forces and train them, holding them in Texas and thus forcing Santa Anna to come across the great distance of desert and mountain? This was Houston's view, but he was willing to make one concession to the Matamoros plan. He would reduce the project to a raid in force, a blow that would damage the place as a base and throw possible Mexican preparations off balance. For this purpose Houston, as commander in chief, appointed a man he could trust, Jim Bowie. But before word could be sent to Bowie, things were hopelessly muddled.

The Matamoros project had split the Texas government wide open. The Governor supported Houston, but the Council ignored him and Bowie and appointed another man to command the expedition. Then, to make matters worse, they appointed still another commander, without revoking their first appointment. For final confusion Dr. Grant laid claim to command. Without any authority, he had already stripped the Alamo of such men as he could lure away, of

food and medical supplies, and even of some of its
cannon.

There was now grave doubt that Texas should try
to hold Bexar and the Alamo. It was true that the
San Antonio River did make a good natural defense
line, with Bexar as the anchor at one end and Goliad
at the other. But the line was strong only if the forti-

fications at each end were strong. And the word Houston was getting from Bexar was not encouraging. The commander there, a Colonel Neill, a man whom Houston trusted, wrote that his men were almost naked. They had not been paid, and they talked of going home. Moreover, he couldn't get horses for scouting and so lay blind, with the approach of a Mexican army more likely every day.

No wonder Houston was in doubt about holding the Alamo. Meanwhile, he had ordered Bowie there with some thirty men, suggesting that they blow up the Alamo and retire north with what cannon and supplies they could carry. Presumably this was a mere suggestion, not an absolute order. If the orders had been absolute, would Houston have sent in the additional thirty men with Bowie? In any case, Bowie and Neill made up their minds to stay. There was the argument that they couldn't get enough stock to move the cannon and supplies. But the real reason may have been in a letter of February 2, 1836, which Bowie wrote to Governor Smith: "Colonel Neill and myself have come to the solemn resolution that we will rather die in these ditches than give it up to the enemy."

They had picked their ground. Nobody was making them stay there.

Buck Travis, now Lieutenant Colonel Travis, had also been ordered down to the Alamo. He was an ambitious, hot-tempered, red-headed man, and he did not like the order that would put him in a post where he would be outranked by a big name like Bowie, or even Neill. It might reduce his chances for fame and promotion. He protested the order, but in the end he was enough of a soldier to obey it. He led in some thirty men with him. By February 3rd he was there.

Other men were arriving. There was Bonham, a young lieutenant of cavalry and old school friend of Travis, who had just come to Texas the previous December. Houston had already said of Bonham that he "ought to be made a major by all means." There was also a young physician, a Dr. Sutherland from Alabama.

10

The Long Rifle Comes In

ON FEBRUARY 11TH ANOTHER MAN ARRIVED, A MAN TO
be more famous than either Bonham or Sutherland.
He was, in fact, already as famous as Bowie. Even
when this man wore ordinary clothes he was a figure
to attract attention, for he was tall and big at a
time when men generally did not grow as big as they
do today. But he did not always wear ordinary
clothes. He might appear with his head covered with
a coonskin cap, tail attached. He might wear buckskin breeches and buckskin coat with buttons whit-

tled from horn. If the weather blew up cold he might have a scarf of fur over his shoulders. On his feet were moccasins.

Not only was he big, he was handsome as well. His nose was big and well shaped, and although his face was reddish and weathered, it was clean-cut with high cheekbones. His hair was darkish brown. The eyes were blue, or gray-blue—the eye color of the great marksmen. The face could break into a ready grin, a grin that made other men want to laugh, too. Or he could keep his face straight while he told some outrageous, incredible tale. Then when other men began laughing, his own face would remain as straight as a hickory shingle. That made the tale sound all the funnier.

The man's name was, of course, Davy Crockett. There was nobody else like him in the world. He was the hero of all the frontier country, the greatest tale teller and bear killer. He was a ringtail roarer. He could grin a coon out of a high hickory on a moonlight night. He was half horse and half alligator. He fanned himself with a hurricane, wore a cast-iron shirt, picked his teeth with a pitch fork, and snored so loud he had to sleep in another house to keep from waking himself up. He could slide down the slippery end of a rainbow and wring the tail off a comet if it came too close. He was the "yaller" blossom of the forest and the pride of humankind. He was, in short, a legend already.

He was a legend, but he was also a real man, leading a little group of Tennesseans into the Alamo.

Jim Bowie had come to the Alamo with that knife that could tickle a man's ribs a long time without making him laugh. Davy Crockett brought his long rifle—his "Betsy," which without firing a shot could make a coon climb down out of a tree. Yes, even the coons had heard what Davy and his Betsy could do. So when Davy went hunting, the coon, as like as not, would just call down, "Is that you, Davy?"

And when Davy said yes, the coon said: "All right, don't shoot. I'll be right down."

The coon had heard about the long rifle and what it could do. But Santa Anna had not heard. He did not know that the pellet of a long rifle could take the eye out of a squirrel in the top of a hickory tree. Or that at a hundred paces it could peck into the point where two lines crossed to make a target on a clean shingle. That rifle was a big part of American history.

Davy Crockett led the Tennesseans into the Alamo.

It had filled the belly with bear meat. It had put buckskin on the back and coonskin on the head of generations of frontiersmen. It had knocked the Cherokee off the Tennessee River and the Shawnee out of the meadows of Kentucky. It had knocked the British into the sea. But Santa Anna had not heard, apparently, of the battle of King's Mountain or of New Orleans, and what the rifle could do.

A Crockett had been at the battle of King's Mountain, carrying a long rifle. After the British surrender he had gone west into the valley of the Nolackucky, in Tennessee. This had been the strong country of the Cherokees, and there were still wandering bands of Indians about. Such a band fell on the Crockett cabin and killed the family. But not long after, in August, 1786, a child was born in another Crockett cabin a few miles away. He was named David Crockett, for the grandfather the Indians had just killed.

Like Houston and Bowie, Davy Crockett was a child of the wilderness. When he was eight years old, he was stout enough to hold a rifle. It was longer than he was tall, and a little boy's arms couldn't hold it steady for long. However, he didn't have to hold it steady for long; he had to hold it steady just long enough. There were men who could shoot the wick out from under a candle flame and not spill any grease. There were men who could cut the string of a kite in a high wind. That was the kind of marksman Davy meant to be.

By the time Davy came to Texas he had been many things. He had been a scout and soldier under Andrew Jackson in the same campaign against the Indians in which Houston had served. Like Houston he had made a name for himself. He had been a scratch farmer of the frontier, planting his corn among the burned trees. He had been the most famous hunter of his time, and people even knew the names of his bear dogs—Holdfast, Growler, Deathmaul and Grim. He had been a colonel of militia. There was a play about him as the perfect frontiersman, and a book about him. He had written a book himself, the story of his life and the life of the frontier. He had been a congressman.

In Congress he had opposed President Jackson's policy of driving the Indians west. He thought that this broke a treaty with them. "It is not justice," he said. "I would rather be an old coon dog belonging to a poor man in the forest than belong to a party that will not do justice to all." But it was dangerous to oppose Jackson, and so in the end Davy failed to be sent back to Congress.

In November, 1835, Davy left Tennessee. According to a book that claimed to be a diary of his journey into Texas, he rode across the country with a strange and raffish set of companions he had picked up on the way—a bee hunter, a gambler off a river boat, a pirate, and an Indian. Davy may have taken up with some such strange companions on his leisurely journey across Texas, but by the time he got to the Alamo, they were no longer with him. The people he had with him there were of another cut—a mixed lot of frontiersmen, doctors, and lawyers—all drawn down toward the little spot in Texas where the trouble was. Most of the men with him were Tennesseans.

Davy was well received at the Alamo. The men there knew who he was, that he would be a good man in a tight squeeze, a cool one in the clutch. They wanted to make him a colonel. He would be just a kind of high private, he said. He may have been just a kind of high private, but the Tennesseans stuck with him and looked to him for orders. Davy Crockett had come to Texas for a fresh start. "In hopes," he said, "of making a fortune for myself and family." But before he could start making the fortune he would have to help take care of the trouble at the Alamo. It was now the end of the first week in February, 1836. Everybody knew that trouble was coming. It was just a question of when and how much.

11

The Gates Are Closed:
Victory or Death

THEY WERE ALL THERE NOW, IN THE WALLS OF THE
Alamo, waiting—Bowie, Travis, Bonham, Crockett,
Sutherland, and the others. But as far as the rest of
Texas was concerned, they might have already been
dead and forgotten. The factions in the government
were still wrapped up in their personal spites and
rivalries. No supplies or reinforcements came to the
Alamo. The soldiers, at least those who might have
helped the Alamo, were almost as bad or as stupid.
Over at Goliad Colonel Fannin had 400 men, the big-

gest Texas force. He, however, was deaf to appeals, even when a message said that the Mexicans were really approaching. And Houston had no men or supplies to send.

As for Dr. Grant, he was still making ready for his Matamoros project. But that great project had dwindled. There was a raid for horses which wound up in a Texas norther with several of Grant's men and most of the horses frozen to death. Then there was another raid for horses down near Matamoros, but this time there was something worse than a norther. Dr. Grant rode right into an ambush and a general slaughter. He was one of the victims.

Thus the men in the Alamo were alone. But that was not the worst thing. The lack of authority in the state was reflected here, too. The men refused to drill or, if some of the regulars did consent to drill, they did it in a half-hearted way, a sort of grudging concession to their officers. As for the volunteers, they simply wouldn't drill. They had come to fight. Drilling was beneath their dignity, and the idea of patching up fortifications was unthinkable.

So regulars and volunteers alike spent most of their time snoozing in the shade, going to cockfights in the town in the daytime and to dances and fandangos at night. They courted the girls, bullied respectable citizens, and now and then appropriated a piece of attractive property.

Colonel Neill was called away on urgent family business. His departure finished the job of destroying respect for authority. Travis now came into command of the regulars, but Neill knew that the volunteers, who considerably outnumbered the regulars, would not accept his command. So Neill arranged for the election of a commander of volunteers. Bowie was the logical and overwhelming choice. But now a question arose about the relative authority of Bowie and Travis. In the general confusion Travis threatened to withdraw from the fort to Medina, a few miles off, and Bowie got drunk and released military prisoners. The men lost the last shreds of discipline.

But Travis and Bowie were, after all, men of character and judgment and a sense of duty, and so they eventually overcame their ambitious rivalries. By this time, the middle of February, word of the approach of the Mexican army had come in. The Texans had no proper scouting service—perhaps because men wouldn't take orders to go on patrol. A young Mexican officer of the Texas garrison at the Alamo, Captain Juan Seguin, sent out his own nephew to spy on the army of Santa Anna. When the nephew got back with the news of the approaching army, some of the officers may have believed him, but most of the garrison put it down as "Mexican lies."

However, the Mexican citizens of Bexar believed the news. Very quietly, those who had the means began loading carts and leaving town. They had been present at one battle and they didn't want to be around for the next one.

But this exodus did not impress the garrison. They trusted themselves. And probably it was just as well, for the Alamo was certainly not much of a fortification to trust. It had been designed and built for protection of the Franciscans against marauding Indians, and it could serve that purpose well enough. But now it was to be besieged by an army trained in assault and supported by fieldpieces, if not by proper siege guns. Against such a force the Alamo was as much of a trap as a defense.

We know very well what it was like. At the time the last battle was going on at the Alamo, there lived over at Matamoros a retired United States Army officer named Potter. After the war was over he inspected the spot and left a careful military description of it. Here is his drawing:

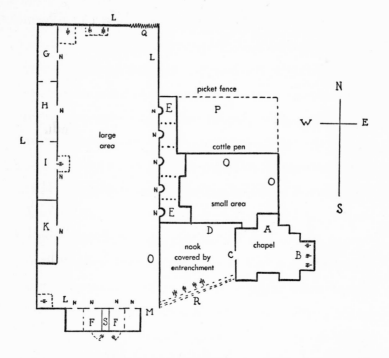

Plan of Alamo based on Captain R. M. Potter's sketch.

(A) chapel (B) apse (C) doorway (D) wall connecting chapel and long barracks (E) long barracks (F) south barracks (G, H, I, K) separate stone rooms (L) walls of old mission plaza (M) main gateway (N) doors to barracks and store rooms (O) low stone walls (P) cattle pen (Q) breach made by artillery (R) entrenchment and earthworks (S) porte-cochere (◼) indication of cannon

The main part of the defense was the plaza of the old mission, which lay north and south. This had stone walls two feet and nine inches thick and nine to twelve feet high on the exposed parts. At the southeast corner, however, where to the east lay the area covered by the earth fortifications, the wall was only four feet high. The length of the plaza was 150 yards, the width 54 yards. On the inside of the west wall, we see indicated some rooms with doors opening out into the plaza, and on the east wall, five doors opening into the two-story barracks built between the plaza on one side and the cattle pen and small area on the other. At the south end, there were more barracks, 114 feet long and 17 feet deep, divided by a kind of porte-cochere. All the buildings had heavy, flat cement roofs laid on timbers. The chapel was more solidly built than most of the place, and the area in front was fortified by earth packed between two palisade fences. The walls of the area to the north of this were, however, very low and weak, and the cattle pen had only a paling fence.

The walls weren't heavy enough to withstand protracted artillery fire, even from the light fieldpieces which the Mexicans might bring with them. But what strength the walls did have couldn't be properly used by the defenders. There were very few loopholes and a man had to stand on a platform behind the wall, or on a mound of earth, to get off his fire. So his head and chest were exposed to the enemy. The men had preferred fandangos to the work of cutting loopholes through almost three feet of stone wall.

The stituation was about as bad for the defending artillery. The defenders had to run their cannon up on mounds built behind the walls and fire over them with very little protection. There were no outworks of any kind; the attackers could march up on un-obstructed level ground. There had not even been any attempt to demolish certain buildings of the town which would give cover to attackers.

As for weapons inside the fort, there were only fourteen serviceable cannon, smooth bore, muzzle-loading pieces, all of them very small for use in forti-fication. For small arms the men had the long rifles with the flintlocks, some newer rifles with percussion caps instead of flint, and an assortment of pistols which included gamblers' derringers and double-bar-reled horse pistols. Then there were also hunting knives, bowie knives (including Jim Bowie's own), and Arkansas toothpicks, which were long, tapering, straight-bladed heavy knives for stabbing or throwing. There were even a few tomahawks, a weapon many frontiersmen found handy. And a few officers had swords.

As for man power, there were about 170 soldiers. Toward the end, 32 more men, heroic volunteers from Gonzales, managed to get in. They brought the total to around 200, but there was a big list of sick and of men not yet recovered from wounds received back in December, probably some 20 odd. This would give about 180 men for active defense. In addition, there were ten or twelve women, including the wife of Lieutenant Dickenson, a number of small children, some Mexican refugees from Bexar, and two Negro slave boys who belonged to Travis and Bowie.

Who were these men, the unknown men who were going to die soon, along with the famous men like Travis and Bowie and Crockett? A large number of the Texans who had captured the Alamo from General Cos back in December had by now gone home, or headed off to their deaths near Matamoros with

Doctor Grant. Their places had been taken by volunteers, men from the United States who had come down after the actual fighting started. Some had come down individually or in small groups, some with military organization, like the New Orleans Grays.

More than half of the men were from the South, with Tennessee furnishing the biggest single group, twenty-nine men. More than twenty men came from the North. There were many foreigners; almost forty men from Great Britain (including eleven Irishmen), a few Germans, and a lone Dane. There were nine Mexicans, men like Captain Juan Seguin, who felt themselves Texans and defenders of the old republican rights of the Mexican Constitution of 1824.

Within these groups there were, certainly, many kinds of men. Some were desperadoes and some were idealists, but most were in between these extremes. There were a few traits they would have had in common. They were men who could take risks. They were men who had a thirst for adventure. They were men with gambling blood. And most of them had had some experience with frontier life. They knew the frontier code and they knew the frontier weapons. This would be true even of most of the professional men, lawyers and doctors, who came to Texas—the type of Travis and Houston and Bonham.

When Captain Juan Seguin's nephew rode in with his news that on Februray 18th the Mexican army had crossed the Rio Grande and was already at Laredo, ready for the thrust northward, few Texans believed him. They didn't believe the report even when the Mexicans of Bexar began to load their carts and pour out of town. Then came a message from another friendly Mexican that a large force was at Leon, only eight miles out, and would have hit the Texans by surprise if a rainstorm hadn't bogged them down. When this message came, a fandango was going on. The scribbled note was put in Bowie's hand, and Bowie sought out Travis. But Travis was too busy entertaining a girl, so nothing was done.

Even on the morning of February 23rd, when the flight of the Mexicans from Bexar was so marked that nobody could ignore it, the Texans were still not convinced of the truth of the "Mexican lies." But Travis did order Doctor Sutherland to put a man on the roof of the old church to ring the bell if he saw anything.

The bell rang, a crowd gathered before the church, Travis among them, and men climbed up to look. There was nothing to see. The sentinel swore that he had seen something, that the force he had spied had now gone behind a growth of brush. No, this was only another big lie. No use to get excited.

Dr. Sutherland was no soldier, but he did have a soldierly idea. Instead of jawing all day, why not send out a scout? He even volunteered to go himself if somebody who knew the country would go with him. A brave man, John W. Smith, said he would go, and so they set out toward Leon. Of course, there would be no Mexican army, but if there should be they would return at a dead run. That could be taken as a signal by the watchman on the church.

Only a mile and a half out of town, Dr. Sutherland crested a ridge, and there below him, only 150 yards off, was the Mexican cavalry—1,500 men, the sun bright on their gear and polished breastplates. They were being ranged in the mesquite and chaparral, with their commander riding along the line, his sword lifted in the sunlight.

Long after, Dr. Sutherland said it was a thrilling sight. But now he did not linger to admire it. He and Smith started off at a dead run.

The rain that had bogged down the Mexican advance and saved Bexar from surprise now in a strange way was to save the life of Dr. Sutherland. On a slick

Dr. Sutherland's horse slipped and threw him.

109

slope, his running horse slipped and threw the rider, and then fell across his legs. Smith helped the doctor remount, but when they rode into Bexar with the news and Dr. Sutherland tried to dismount, his knees buckled under him. This injury was to mean that he would not be in the Alamo for the finish.

When Sutherland and Smith dashed into the plaza of Bexar, Travis was already pulling back into the fortress, trying to make ready at this last minute for the crisis. He knew that he needed more men, needed them desperately. He sent off another appeal to Fannin at Goliad. And even as Sutherland was giving his report, Travis asked the doctor to ride to Gonzales, some sixty miles off, and see if he could raise help. Then Crockett, who happened to be standing by, said to Travis: "Colonel, here I am. Assign me a position, and the Tennessee boys will try to hold it." So for his first assignment Crockett drew the cattle pen.

The troops were back now in the main structure of the Alamo. Food had been running short, but as they were pulling back in from the town, they had encountered a big herd of cattle being driven into town. (We don't know whose cattle they were, but from that time on their home was the Alamo.) The troops also had the luck to find a good supply of corn in the houses abandoned by fleeing citizens. As for water, they didn't want to depend on the little canal just beyond the walls, which was exposed to Mexican fire. They dug a well inside. The dirt was of some use, too. It helped make a mound to mount cannon.

Toward four o'clock Sutherland rode out of the Alamo with Smith, bound for Gonzales. As they forded the river, the doctor sat astride his horse and watched, not far off, the Mexican army moving into the plaza of Bexar in grand order, with flags and music. Then Sutherland and Smith were off toward Gonzales.

They stopped once to buy some gourds from an old Mexican for use as canteens, then stopped again to fill the gourds before striking away from water. Sutherland now was in great pain, and said he had better go back. But in the distance they heard the sound of full cannonade. The Alamo must be surrounded by now, Smith said, and Sutherland wouldn't be able to get back in.

Smith and Sutherland reached Gonzales the next afternoon, February 24th, and men began rallying for the Alamo. But they had to organize and make preparation before starting out. Besides, they expected other men to come in from farther off, to make a strong relief force.

Every morning, well before dawn, messengers from Gonzales rode out toward Bexar. Travis had agreed on a signal to show that he still held out. At dawn, every day, he would fire his big eighteen-pounder. The scouts would ride out to the Cibolo, lay ear to the ground, and strain to catch the far boom that would seem to swell out of the earth.

By the middle of the afternoon when the Mexicans first marched into Bexar, they were setting up their batteries across the river on the edge of town. Yonder a red flag was running up over the church in Bexar, the San Fernando. The red flag was Santa Anna's and it meant *No Quarter*.

The Alamo made answer with a shot from its heaviest gun, the eighteen-pounder.

Then a white flag unexpectedly ran up over the Mexican lines, and a bugle sounded. This time, unlike the morning in the Bexar plaza back in December, the Texans knew what the bugle call meant. It was the call to parley.

After their dispute, Bowie and Travis had agreed to take joint command of the Texan army. But this call to parley at the moment of crisis almost split the command again. Travis wanted to ignore the call. But Bowie, not consulting him, sent out a messenger under a white flag, asking the intention of the parley. The messenger's letter wound up with the words "God

The parley upset the relations between Travis and Bowie.

and Texas!" indicating how little Bowie himself was inclined to surrender.

The messenger brought back a letter from Santa Anna's aide. It stated that the Mexican army would not "come to terms under any conditions with rebellious foreigners to whom there was no recourse left, if they wished to save their lives, than to place themselves immediately at the disposal of the Supreme Government." This was presumably a more polite and long-winded way of saying no quarter. Except that in this case death would be slower and later, by rope or firing squad.

A little later a Mexican soldier walked casually across an open space in the town. He was, he quite naturally assumed, out of range. There was a little whiff of smoke from the Alamo, the tiny tap of the report in the distance, and the calm Mexican soldier was dead. The tale in Texas was that Davy Crockett gave that first exhibition in marksmanship. He was just keeping his hand in, showing the boys how.

The business of the parley had upset the relations between the joint commanders. Travis was angry.

And Bowie was not a man to take things too meekly. As the men settled down for the night and the long grim pull of a siege, they knew that their commanders were again at outs. This would mean a deep split in loyalty, right down the middle of the garrison.

But here accident took a hand. A little earlier, Bowie, in directing the placing of a cannon, had slipped from a scaffold and taken a bad fall. On February 23rd, the day of the Mexican advance, he was able to be about, though with a temper probably not much improved by his injuries. The next day he had a roaring fever. He knew he was a sick man. He called the garrison together and formally passed over the full command to Travis.

Travis had not wanted to come to the Alamo in the first place. Outranked by both Bowie and Neill, he had feared that he wouldn't get promotion and fame. Now he was in full command. That was better than a formal promotion. And he did not have to wait much longer for his fame.

Travis had the air of a man who was expecting fame. He saw himself standing at the heroic moment. He knew the language of fame. The next day he wrote a famous letter:

COMMANDANCY OF THE ALAMO
Bexar, Feby. 24, 1836.

To the People of Texas and All Americans in the world—Fellow Citizens and Compatriots: I am besieged with a thousand or more of the Mexicans under Santa Anna. I have sustained a continual Bombardment and cannonade for 24 hours and have not lost a man. The enemy has demanded a surrender at discretion; otherwise, the garrison are to be put to the sword, if the fort is taken. I have answered the demand with a cannon shot, and our flag still waves proudly from the walls. *I shall never surrender or retreat.* Then I call upon you in the name of Liberty, of patriotism, and everything dear to the American character, to come to our aid with all dispatch. The enemy is receiving reinforcements daily and will no doubt increase to three or four thousand in four or five days. If this call is neglected, I am determined to sustain myself as long as possible and die like a soldier who never forgets what is due his own honor and that of his country. VICTORY OR DEATH.

WILLIAM BARRET TRAVIS
Lt. Col. Comdt.

"Our flag still waves proudly from the walls," wrote Travis in the letter his messenger took out for help. The help Travis seemed to be thinking about was help from Americans for Americans. But the flag flying over the southwest corner of the Alamo was still the Mexican tricolor—red, white, and green. Instead of the eagle in the white bar, the defenders had the number 1824. This stood for the Mexican Constitution of 1824, which had been overthrown by Santa Anna, and under which the defenders were now claiming by their flag the rights of loyal citizens of the state of Texas of the republic of Mexico.

But the rights of Mexican citizens were probably not much in the mind of Travis. Nor in the minds of a number of Texans who, at that very moment, in the little settlement of Washington in the Austin grant, were gathered in a convention to debate the matter of independence for Texas.

117

12

A Sword Point and a Line
in the Dust

WHILE THE CONVENTION DEBATED OVER AT WASHINGTON, the men at the Alamo settled down to the routine of the siege. They assumed, naturally, that help would come from somewhere. All they had to do was to hold on till it came and pin down Santa Anna until Texas could be organized for a final struggle. Meanwhile, the Mexican artillery kept up a continual bombardment during the day. The men in the fort had to serve their own cannon and try to prevent the Mexicans from placing or advancing batteries. The riflemen had to keep watch for any target that might indiscreetly present itself over there. And after midnight on the second night, the first of the night sorties was made to destroy some sheds too close to the walls and bring in wood for cookfires and scaffolding.

On the third day, February 25th, the Mexicans tried to close in. They brought their headquarters across the river and tried to set up a battery directly in front of the gate of the Alamo. The Texan fire was too hot, and the Mexicans pulled back with some losses. But after dark they could take advantage of earlier Texan shiftlessness. Some buildings that should have been torn down gave cover between the Alamo and the river. With this protection the Mexicans managed to set up guns only 300 yards from the gate, too close for comfort. Though the Texans did break out during the night and burn some wooden buildings that had given cover, the main damage was already done. When dawn came the new batteries were in place. And Mexican cavalry was close enough to skirmish with some Texans outside the walls. What was more disturbing, the Mexican cavalry had swung eastward across the Gonzales road.

It was cold now, really cold, for a norther had blown up. This day passed like the day before with bombardment from the Mexican cannon. With some of the wood they had brought in, the Texans were putting up scaffolding for sharpshooters inside the old chapel. The Mexicans tried to cut off the Alamo from water, not knowing, we guess, of the well in the fort. They also managed to push up another battery. In the afternoon heavy reinforcements arrived in the Mexican camp.

Then night settled down. The defenders knew that the Mexican sentinels were working in closer, the lines tightening. The Texans made another sortie and burned more buildings that might be useful as cover for attackers. The cannon fire from the besiegers stopped, began again, stopped, began, with a nerve-fraying irregularity. The watchmen strained from the walls. They were sleepy.

Fannin must have had the message by now. He would come soon, they were sure. With four hundred fresh men they might show Santa Anna something. Then a man could get some sleep.

And so it went—new batteries pushing closer, the sentinels working in closer, Mexican entrenchments cutting in closer. New reinforcements were arriving over yonder; the tempo of bombardment was mounting. This meant night alarms, no sleep. The Texans had to go easy on their own cannon now. Ammunition wouldn't last forever, and they knew they would need it worse later. They would need it when the Mexicans massed for the assault.

It had been a week since the siege began and word went out to Fannin. Bonham had slipped out of the fort two days before to hurry him, and the besieged Texans were expecting the arrival of Fannin's troops. Excitement was in the fort. But night fell and Fannin still hadn't come. So Travis ordered out Captain Juan Seguin to meet him, to hurry him. Seguin had no horse. He went to borrow Bowie's. Bowie was so deep now in his fever that he scarcely recognized Seguin.

Since the last messengers had not returned, there was now the terrible thought that Mexican patrols had picked them up. But Seguin could get through if anybody could. He was a Mexican, he could fool the patrols. He took one man with him, the nephew who had played spy on Santa Anna's approaching army and had got called a liar for his pains.

It was just as well that it was Seguin, the Mexican, who went as the messenger. Not far out he was hailed by a Mexican cavalry patrol. He was smart enough not to make a break for it, and when he answered, his reply was in the language that lulled suspicion. Seguin and his nephew rode casually toward the approaching patrol, the patrol they would have to pass. When they were abreast of the patrol they suddenly drove in the spurs, leaned far over to make poor marks for pistol fire, and fled. The patrol was taken by surprise and had to wheel from a standing start. Their bullets missed. The two horses outran the Mexican cavalry, then lost them in woodland.

But it was all to be in vain. Fannin had already had the message. He had actually started out for the Alamo, but in a strange, half-hearted, aimless way. When a supply wagon broke down just a few miles out of Goliad, he changed his mind and marched back to Goliad. Near Goliad, Seguin met one of Fannin's officers and heard the story. He turned and rode for Gonzales. Perhaps help could be had there.

When Seguin arrived at Gonzales he found that the relief party had already left for the Alamo. After the first news from Sutherland and Smith, the Gonzales men had made their preparations and waited for the Texas relief expedition to rally. But Texas did not rally. So the men of Gonzales—thirty-two of them —finally marched away on their own. They knew that thirty-two men could do nothing to change the situation against Santa Anna's thousands, but they did what they had to do to keep their own self-respect. They couldn't just sit quietly some sixty miles away and not lift a finger.

After dark, the night of March 1st, these men approached Bexar with John W. Smith, the earlier companion of Dr. Sutherland, as guide. On the outskirts of the settlement, they suddenly encountered a shadowy figure, a horseman, in the darkness. In perfect English the horseman asked, "Do you want to go into the fort, gentlemen?"

"Yes," one of the Gonzales men replied.

"Then follow me," the shadowy figure said, and wheeled his horse and led them toward the dark town.

But Smith didn't like it. He didn't like it a bit. It just didn't feel right. "Boys," he said softly, "it's time to be after shooting that fellow."

The strange horseman must have had ears like a lynx and split-second reflexes. The words weren't out of Smith's mouth before the stranger had set spur and, leaping into the dark brush by the track, was gone. The Gonzales men weren't a trigger-slow kind, but the stranger was quicker.

Who was he? Nobody ever knew for sure, but the guess was that he was General Adrian Woll, an Englishman who had adventured into the Mexican army.

Smith now sent a scout ahead to make contact with the sentries of the Alamo. He knew that the men on the walls, sleepless, with nerves worn thin, and fearful of a surprise attack at night, would be inclined to shoot first and ask questions later. He was right. Even with the precaution of an advance scout, one sentry let off a shot when the main body approached. There was, fortunately, only one nervous sentry, and the rifle ball, fortunately, found only a foot.

So the Gonzales men were in. It must have meant something to the men in the fort, after eight days of battle and dwindling hope, to have friends suddenly ride in out of the dark. They had not been forgotten after all.

It was just as well that the Gonzales men made the fort by the night of March 1st. The next day

Santa Anna discovered a concealed road leading to the Alamo and posted a battalion to cut it off. This must have been the road used by the Gonzales men.

Santa Anna may have thought that he had cut the last line of communication between the Alamo and the outside world, but he hadn't. At eleven o'clock on the morning of March 3rd, men on the walls could see a horseman making a dash for the Alamo gates, leading a Mexican patrol by a fair margin. It was Bonham. In broad daylight he had sneaked through the Mexican lines—how, only the Lord knew —and then had trusted his horse and his horsemanship for the dash past the patrols.

Bonham had gone out with the second appeal to Fannin. He had ridden some three hundred miles in four and a half days, had taken his chances with the Mexicans both going and coming. He was a tough man, and here he was back. He was back with bad news. Fannin would not come. Nobody else would come.

So Travis wrote his last letter—to the president of the convention meeting over at Washington to debate politics and independence. It was a long letter. He was surrounded, he said, by entrenchments and batteries. "In Bexar, four hundred yards west; in Lavillita, three hundred yards south; at the powder house, one thousand yards east of south; on the ditch, eight hundred yards northeast, and at the old mill, eight hundred yards north." Two hundred shells had fallen in the fort, but he had not lost a man, and many of the enemy were dead. But there were so many more, perhaps as many as 6,000. And as he knew how little chance there was, he wrote: "I will, however, do the best I can under the circumstances; and I feel confident that the determined valor heretofore exhibited by my men will not fail them in the last struggle. The victory will cost the enemy so dear that it will be worse for him than defeat."

Then Travis wrote a letter to a friend. "Take care of my little boy," he begged. "If the country should be saved, I may make him a splendid fortune; but if the country should be lost and I should perish, he will have nothing but the proud recollection that he is the son of a man who died for his country."

Other men in the fort had children. Some of them sat down to write letters, taking a minute or two off

126

the walls or away from the gun mounds or out of the time when they might have tried to catch a wink of sleep. This was the last chance for letters. They knew that.

A messenger went out with the letters, and he made it.

Others might have gone out and made it. Many of the men inside were frontiersmen who knew the tricks of concealment and stealth. But this was the last night to take the chance, for the Mexican lines were drawing closer and closer.

In a lull in the Mexican bombardment, Travis called his men together. He said that there was no hope of help coming and that he would ask no man to stay who wanted to try to escape. Now was the time for each man to make up his mind. Travis drew his sword and with its point he scratched a long line in the dust.

Then he stepped across the line and turned back to face his men. Who would join him?

A few men came right over to Travis. They were the ones who were always ready to take a dare, even with death at the end of it. It has been said

Bonham, leading a Mexican patrol by a fair margin,

that Davy Crockett was the first man over the line. If not the first, he was certainly not the last, for he was of that breed.

There were still some across the line—men who had the moment of natural fear that most of us have, or who simply needed a moment to make up their minds. But there was one man across the line who wasn't afraid and who didn't need any time to make up his mind. If he was still on the wrong side of the line, it was because he couldn't move. He was Jim Bowie, lying on his cot, very sick now with pneumonia.

was making a dash for the Alamo gates.

But it was not going to be said that he would not take a dare.

"Boys," Bowie called out to those who had already crossed over, "I can't make it, but I'll thank you if you give me a hand."

So four came back and picked up the cot and carried him over.

That was enough for those who still hesitated. They all crossed over. That is, all but one.

This was a man named Rose, a Frenchman, once a soldier under Napoleon and now a friend of Jim

Bowie. But he was not at the Alamo to fight. He had come on business and been trapped. So he stood there alone, and the others looked across the line at him.

He sank down and covered his face with his hands. We don't know whether he did it out of shame or fear. But anyway that night the man named Rose, with some dirty clothes done up in a bundle, dropped over the wall and crept away in the darkness. Somewhere in that open space, he got blood on his bundle from the body of one of the Mexicans who had fallen there.

He made his way to the river and waded it at the ford. Then he went through the town, which seemed deserted. The people who remained had barred their doors. He went down the river, along the bank, in a strange stillness. Then the cannonade began again.

Now he was safely through the Mexican lines. The sound of cannon continued as he traveled in the cover of darkness. It was slow going in the dark, and over and over again he stumbled into cactus. His legs were full of thorns that worked deep into the flesh. Three days later, crippled from the thorns and nearly starving, he reached the Guadalupe River. He found an old log, rolled it into the river, then clung to it and kicked and paddled across.

On the bluff on the other side of the Guadalupe he found a house. It was deserted. In fact, the whole country for many miles around was deserted. People had fled in panic from the Mexicans. Here Rose found some food left in the haste of departure. At other abandoned homesteads he had the same luck. So after two or three weeks, desperately sick now from the thorns, he found a family named Zuber that took him in and nursed him. To them he told his story, and the story of how Travis drew the line in the dust with his sword point.

Years later, the Zuber family reported the story of Rose. For a long time nobody believed it. There was no record of a man named Rose who had been at the Alamo. Then it was discovered that in one locality of northeast Texas the courts had accepted the testimony of a man named Rose as to who had been at the Alamo in the last days. So there is some evidence for the existence of Rose and for the story he told of the line in the dust.

There is no evidence, however, for the story that it

Four men came back and carried Jim Bowie across the

line Travis had scratched in the dust with his sword.

was Davy Crockett who helped Rose over the wall. But Davy was the kind of man who would have helped him over the wall and not held it against him, even if Davy knew where he himself belonged. He would have turned from the wall to crack another joke, or pick up an old fiddle and saw out another dancing or breakdown tune, an old-fashioned, backwoods "toe smasher" such as "Old Joe Clark," "Turkey in the Straw," or "Leather Britches."

This was another tale told about Davy, that he fiddled now and then during the siege. He was not much of a fiddler, but his funny fooling with the instrument would have done something to raise the spirits of the men in the lulls between bombardments.

13

Last Blood

THE NIGHT OF MARCH 3RD, THE TEXANS MADE ANOTHER
of their night sallies—to kill Mexicans, to throw an
attack off balance, to show that they were still there.
But the sally did not prevent the Mexicans from moving guns closer. Dawn showed a battery close to
the north wall, and all that day the hammering went
on. The Mexican guns were not heavy siege guns. It
had not been possible to bring that kind of artillery
across the desert and mountains. But even these fieldpieces, at closer and closer range, were having their

effect. The crumbling old stone could not stand that punishment forever.

Nor could human flesh and blood stand it forever. True, nobody had yet been killed in the fort, but under that bombardment and with the constant threat of attack there was no sleep. A man might drop down now and then to snatch a moment in some lull, but that was all. The battle went on with its grinding certainty. By March 5th, the guns had knocked a hole in the north wall of the Alamo, somewhat to the east.

With this breach in the wall, a strange thing happened. The Mexican fire began to fall off. It would rise, then die away. There was the hole in the wall. The defenders could see it, see themselves stripped of the safe stone. Yet nothing happened. It was a strain to watch that open spot and have to wonder and wonder when something would happen.

Meanwhile, an occasional shell dropped into the plaza of the Alamo. Then there would be quiet, then some sound from the Mexican lines. Then silence again. Santa Anna's headquarters were very close now, only a few hundred yards off. There was the red flag floating above the headquarters. The Texans could see it.

Night came on. The firing all but died away. The Texans on the wall dropped down to sleep. They couldn't believe that it was this quiet. Even some of the sentries slept. Travis had sent three sentries out beyond the walls to warn of a night attack. They must have been killed in their sleep. Or perhaps they woke up just at the last instant, under the bayonet point or knife edge.

We know what was happening over in the Mexican camp while the Texans slept. We have Santa Anna's orders for the morning of March 6th, prepared the afternoon before in that strange new quiet.

On March 4th, Santa Anna had had a council of war, a meeting of his colonels and generals. Some of them wanted to wait for heavier artillery and simply knock the walls down, then turn grape shot and canister on the unprotected garrison. Others thought they might risk an assault in a day or two, for troops were coming in and some picked companies had arrived that very day. After all, they had more than 5,000 men now, and they knew the number in the Alamo.

It was not until early the next afternoon, however,

that Santa Anna actually issued his orders. The slow grinding process wasn't fast enough for him. He wanted a flashy victory. It might take a few extra lives, but he had the big margin. The "Napoleon of the West" issued his secret orders to his top command.

The infantry was to be formed in four columns, with the light companies of each battalion and the engineers to be held in reserve. Each column was to be commanded by one of Santa Anna's more trusted and experienced generals or colonels, and he himself would hold the reserve in personal command. Each column was provided with scaling ladders, crowbars, and axes. Santa Anna was very careful in his orders. Men carrying the ladders should sling their guns over the shoulder, and all caps should be provided with chin straps. Bayonets should be put in the best condition, and attacking troops should be abed at sundown to be fresh to use those bayonets before dawn.

Cavalry was ordered to the plaza of Bexar, to be prepared for saddle at 3:00 A.M. The troops were then to take post at various points around the siege lines "to prevent the escape of anyone." "Anyone" probably referred to a few Mexican soldiers who thought a direct assault might be a little like suicide.

All was in readiness. Santa Anna's order read, "His Excellency, the General in Chief, directs that by four o'clock tomorrow morning, the attacking columns shall be stationed within gunshot of the first line of entrenchments for the purpose of making the assault, upon the signal given by His Excellency, which will be the sounding of the bugle of the north battery."

Santa Anna knew the condition of the defenders, their pitiful sleeplessness. He had let them have their last night with no gunfire, no disturbance of any kind. But it was not out of human pity that he let them sleep. Santa Anna knew that once a really tired man sleeps he is hard to wake. Nothing is then so precious as sleep. Inside those Alamo walls the Mexicans' best ally was at work. Sleep.

At 3:00 A.M. there was a little moonlight—not much, but enough for somebody on the wall to catch sight of some motion in the open space toward the Mexican lines. By the time the sentinel had decided that something was really up, there was a sudden shout, a cheer for Santa Anna, and almost immediately from the north battery, the bugle blared the signal for attack. Then there were the shouts of command. The Mexican lines surged forward in solid formation, bayonet points catching the pale moonlight.

Travis heard the first alarm. He leaped up, seized rifle and sword, called for his slave boy Joe, and dashed out into the plaza, shouting to his men, "Come on, boys, the Mexicans are on us!"

He dashed across the plaza to a cannon at the northeast corner, the weak spot, the spot where the wall was breached.

Travis was right, the Mexicans were on them. The Mexican band over yonder where the red flag hung, not yet visible in dawn light, had struck up the *deguello,* the "fire and death" call. That tune, like the red flag, meant no quarter.

The guns of the fort poured their charges of scrap iron and junk into the massed lines, and the riflemen on the walls settled methodically down to their business. The riflemen had one piece of luck. Santa Anna had ordered his artillery not to fire. It might do some damage to his own troops as they closed on the walls.

But the Mexican troops did not close, not this time.

140

The riflemen settled down to their business.

The assault line on the north, where the breach was, wavered and cracked. General Duque, the commander of that column, had taken a mortal wound; but even as he lay on the ground he continued to encourage his men forward. Now, as they broke under the blast of fire from the wall, his men finished the job begun by a Texas bullet. They simply trampled him to death.

The west and east assaults had also failed. The south assault reached the wall and got scaling ladders in place. But those who put foot to them did not live. Then that column broke.

The Texans now had a little breathing space. They had earned it. They could swab their guns and reload. A man could look to his rifle, adjust his flint—if it was a flintlock—or look to the capholder. He could take a little extra care in loading, the craftsman's finickiness. He could take a deep breath. Somebody may have gotten off a grim, tight-jawed joke. Somebody must have looked east as the dawn grew, hoping one last hope that there would be a column of dust there, help coming. But nobody now believed in help.

Did Davy take one last whack at the fiddle, making his racket which was something short of music? Did he yell one last dare to the Mexicans? The Mexicans had seen him on the walls day after day, had learned to identify him—a tall man in buckskin, with long hair and a funny cap. He would get off his shot

with that awful certainty; then, as he calmly reloaded, would yell over to them some words they
didn't understand. "Kwockey," they called him—the
nearest they could come to pronouncing "Crockett."
His fame was now in their lines.

Seeing the last dawn come up, the Texans waited.
They knew it was the last. Well, a man did better
with a little light. With light they could take Jim
Bowie's advice: *shoot to hit.*

The Mexican lines were re-forming, the officers
moving back and forth to dress the lines, to hearten
the men, to insult their manhood, to wave in the dawn
light their own as yet unblooded sword blades. The
Mexicans were soldiers, and they were brave. They
had to be brave to go back again toward the wall.
They could look out there and see what happened in
that space of a hundred yards or so. Those who
had died were lying there beside those who were not
yet dead.

That very night, when all was over, a young private in the Mexican army wrote a letter home, and
told of the assault. "Although the distance was short,"
he wrote, "the fire from the enemy cannon was fearful; we fell back; more than forty men fell around me

in a few moments. One can but admire the stubborn resistance of our enemy and the constant bravery of all our troops. It seemed that every cannon ball or pistol shot of the enemy embedded itself in the breasts of our men, who without stopping cried, 'Long live the Mexican Republic! Long live General Santa Anna!'" And he added that the whole scene was one of "extreme terror."

No, the Mexicans were not cowards. They re-formed the lines, and again there was the blast of the bugle, the music of the *deguello,* there were shouts, and the surge across that blood-streaked space.

It was the same story. The south column again made the wall, then failed to mount. The north column charged in, cracked before the wall, and reeled back. The east and west columns also fell back.

This was the moment when, if at all, the battle hung in the balance. It is conceivable that if, despite the great odds, another assault or two had failed, the troops might have gone sour and the officers themselves might have failed in enthusiasm for suicide. Or worse, they might have gone desperate and tried to lash their men in with the sword-flat. Then, conceivably, Santa Anna might have had to settle down to more siege, to a waiting-out process. And perhaps, *perhaps* things might have been different. Texas might have rallied in time.

But it was not to be that way. We do not know whether what happened next was an accident or whether it was a plan. Anyway, as the attack column fell away from the west wall, it swung to its left, northward; and as the attack column fell away from the east wall, it swung to its right, also to the north. These east and west columns veered northward just in time to strike the retreating north column, fill its depleted ranks, put pressure from the rear on those in front, and drive them forward again while the heat of battle still had a chance to overcome panic. This reinforced, heavier column for the first time hit the wall here. The men wavered, but they had hit the wall. This gave enough confidence for the next try. Meanwhile, the south column had actually thrust some men up the wall at that end. They hadn't lived, but they had been up there. So the second main assault ended.

The Mexicans drew back, but they had learned something. The Texans could see that they were up to something—those among the Texans whose eyes were not too glazed with sleeplessness. It was broad daylight now, but no attack came. The men fell down to take a rest, to doze a moment.

It was full morning before the Mexicans took their old positions. They had now put in the reserves. The defenders pulled themselves together, got back in position. There came the bugle, the music, the shouts and cheers of assault. The north column hung back, but the east and west columns surged forward. These two columns, hit by fire, wavered. But this time their wavering was not, as before, haphazard. They both swung north with some precision. The north column, which had held back, now leaped forward to the attack, and the east and west columns closed in solid behind the attacking north column.

This was the trick. This was what the Mexicans had learned. They had now left the defenders of the east and west walls stranded in the old positions. Only a few, if any, could manage to get over to join the thin line on the north wall in time to take the full weight of the triple attacking column. And certainly no artillery could be shifted.

That triple column of Mexicans took its punishment in the rush to the wall, from the rifle balls and the blast of shot and scrap iron from the cannon. But there were only three cannon being served on this wall, and the space to be crossed by the attackers was not great. Also it took time for the Texans to reload. The rifle fire wasn't heavy enough to stem the rush. The weight of troops from behind drove on over the fallen, and the attack reached the wall. Here, under the wall, the Mexicans were relatively safe, and could collect themselves for the push over.

They were safe there: first, because the defending cannon were set back on mounds inside the walls, and could be used only on troops well out in the open; and second, because a defending rifleman, to get a shot at the enemy below, had to expose himself completely to Mexican fire. As one Mexican officer, General Filisola, later wrote, the men on top of the wall trying to fire down "could not live one second" under the hail of musket balls from the rear ranks of the Mexicans. So the scaling ladders got up, and some of them stuck.

As soon as the Mexicans began to swarm up the ladders, however, the musket fire from their own rear ranks had to slacken, or Mexican slugs would find Mexican flesh. So now the Texans could use again, for a little while anyway, the advantage of the walls. Rifle bullet or pistol bullet could find its target. Then all at once there was no more time to reload; the time had come for gun butt, bowie knife, Arkansas toothpick, clenched fist and bare hand. The wall was narrow, little more than two feet and a half, and the defenders had the drop on the man clambering off his ladder. So here the Texans held.

They held the north wall and the breach in the wall. At the breach the Texans could use rifle fire.

The Mexicans had reached the south wall. But here, too, they were stopped.

This was the last moment of desperate hope and elation. Maybe—maybe—maybe!

But it was not *maybe*. Some of the massed Mexican troops at the north wall had been crowded to the north end of the west wall, overlapping down along it. Somebody—nobody knows who—flung scaling ladders up the west wall. By this time, of course, the defending fighters of the west wall had been drawn over to the north wall. So now the Mexicans made it on the west wall. There just weren't enough Texans to drive them back. Some of the Mexicans died on the

The Mexicans made it on the west wall.

wall but some did not. They dropped over, found their feet, got off a shot and reloaded, or plunged forward with the bayonet.

The main body of the Texans, those on the north wall and those defending the breach, were now hit in the rear. Those on the wall had to drop back in and try to re-form in order to get some purchase for a stand. The walls were free, the breach was free. The Mexicans "poured over like sheep," as Joe, the slave boy of Travis, said after the battle.

There was no chance to organize a defense. There was simply a mad swirl of fighting. The Texans first tried to group along the western walls in front of the stone rooms and barracks there. Then they were squeezed across, or gradually fell back, to the barracks on the east wall and the area in front of the church. In front of the east barracks, they attempted to make a stand, as the piles of dead Mexicans later proved. Meanwhile a few Texans managed to swing the big eighteen-pounder of the west wall around toward the mission plaza and get off a charge of iron into the Mexican mass. Then in the moment of surprise, they managed to reload and fire again. But they had no third try. Mexican musket fire got them, and the desperate and now clearly hopeless struggle continued. There was not even much chance to load now. They fought with clubbed rifle, knife, chunks of stone grabbed from the ground, or bare hands.

The Texans divided, some into the barracks, some into the church area. In the barracks, the Mexicans had to fight up the stairs, and there it was a room-to-room struggle. Around each door lay a heap of dead or dying Mexicans; inside the door, two or three dead Texans. In the large room that had been used as a hospital the Texans held off the enemy until the Mexicans got one of the Alamo's own cannon and at point-blank range blasted the last defenders.

The small area in front of the church, which had been defended by the Tennesseans, held on a little longer. Then the survivors and others fell back into the church itself and barred the doors. They had rifles on the walls and the doors were stout, and they fought here under the eyes of the women and children. But the doors broke and the riflemen were knocked off the wall. It was over.

Texans had planned to set fire to the powder stored

They fought with clubbed rifle, knife, chunks

of stone grabbed from the ground, or bare hands.

in the church and blow everything and everybody to destruction. A Major Robert Evans had tried to fire the magazine, but was killed in the attempt.

Travis was killed at his post, at one of the cannon of the north wall. When he died the cannon was already useless and he was on the point of firing his rifle. A Mexican pistol ball hit him in the head.

There is a little uncertainty about the spot and circumstance of the death of Crockett. Even some of the eye-witness accounts, or accounts that claim to be eye-witness, don't agree. One account says that at the last Crockett holed up in a room. It declares that, one by one, with his clubbed rifle, he brained the Mexicans who tried to enter, until a lucky shot broke his right arm. Then he drew his knife and rushed upon the attackers to get another one or two before he fell. Another account likewise puts "Kwockey" in a room, but his weapons are reversed. It says he guarded the door with his knife—not a clubbed rifle—until hit in the right arm by a Mexican bullet. Upon being hit, he seized his rifle in his left hand and leaped to the middle of the room for space to swing it. But he was now open for a Mexican volley, and fell. However, it seems more likely that he died, with two Tennesseans, near the gate at the wall between the church and the barracks, with some seventeen dead Mexicans grouped there. At least Mrs. Dickenson, the wife of a lieutenant who died in the Alamo, reported that she saw Crockett's body there, "his peculiar cap by his side."

There is also some confusion about the death of Bowie. During most of the siege his cot had been in a room of the barracks, away from the other sick, where he was taken care of by his own men. But toward the end, he was carried into the church and put in a small room at the southwest corner of the building. Here, according to the best evidence, the Mexicans found him. He was a very sick man, but not too sick to summon up some last strength and some last flicker of the old deadliness that had made his name what it was. He had two loaded pistols and his knife, and he did not die alone. After his death, in a vengeful fury, the Mexicans tossed his body on bayonets like a bundle of hay.

Perhaps the last man to die in the fort was Jacob Walker, a gunner who had been on the church wall and at the last had fled to the little room where the women and children were. There by Mrs. Dickenson's side, pleading for his life, he was bayoneted. According to one Mexican account, five other men were found hidden under some mattresses and were dragged out, alive, to Santa Anna. The General rebuked the captors for being chicken-hearted and turned away while they did their work.

The red flag had been flying for thirteen days. The *deguello* had sounded for each attack on that last morning and Santa Anna had given orders for no quarter. The Mexican troops had been slaughtered by hundreds by those defenders who simply wouldn't die and be done with it, and the Mexicans were now inflamed with vengefulness. Even after all the defenders were dead, the blood-orgy continued, finally ending from weariness or under the protests of some of the officers.

One officer, General Filisola, was to write of the morning: "It was a source of deep regret, that after the excitement of the combat, many acts of atrocity were allowed which are unworthy of the gallantry and resolution with which this operation had been executed." He added that many felt only "disgust and horror," and wished for themselves and for the honor of the Mexican Republic that the events had not taken place. Filisola, by the way, had opposed the no-quarter policy, and felt that only Santa Anna's vanity had prevented his giving an opportunity to the Texans to surrender on terms. Would they have taken such an opportunity?

The women and children in the fort, the two slave boys (Bowie's Sam and Travis's Joe), and a Mexican named Anselmo Bogarra, who claimed to have been a servant to Travis, were spared. Mrs. Dickenson, after she had been wounded in the leg, was taken to Santa Anna's headquarters and was well treated. There is even an account that the General wanted to adopt her little girl, Angelina. The mother angrily refused the offer, but was allowed to stay for a few days before she set out for Gonzales. Meanwhile Bogarra had already arrived in Gonzales, bearing news that in that settlement alone there were now thirty-two widows and a hundred fatherless children.

The Texans had lost some 200 men, including the nine of Mexican blood. The Mexican loss was enormous, though the exact number is somewhat uncertain. Santa Anna, of course, lied in his report, saying that more than 600 Texans were killed and only 70 Mexicans, with 300 wounded. There are, however, some fairly good estimates. The Mexican mayor of Bexar, an eyewitness of the fall of the Alamo, was assigned the work of disposing of the bodies of the slain of both sides. He reported that 182 Texans were killed, and more than 1,500 Mexicans of "the flower of the army." Substantiating this figure, there is the report of Dr. Sutherland, whose bad leg had kept him out of the Alamo. As a military doctor, he was present when, some weeks later, after their capture, Santa Anna and his secretary were being questioned about the losses at the Alamo. The secretary admitted 1,600 killed, and Santa Anna did not contradict him. Some historians put the figure down to around 1,000.

There were also a number of wounded to be considered among the losses of effective men, and we must remember that the losses were from the best troops. For example, one battalion of the best troops —one which took part in the last assaults and bore the brunt of the attack on the north wall—lost 670 men out of its full strength of 800. Santa Anna did pick up about 1,000 Mexican recruits in Texas, but they were not trained and could not make up his real losses. His army had blunted its cutting edge. Travis had said, in his last letter out of the Alamo, that if the Mexicans won, it would be for them a victory more costly than a defeat. Travis had made good his boast.

When it came to disposing of the bodies of the slain, the mayor of Bexar, on order of Santa Anna, took a body of cavalry and went to the woods for a great quantity of firewood and kindling. By three o'clock in the afternoon of the day of the fall of the Alamo, the wood was assembled. Three great pyres had been built: first a layer of kindling, then a layer of wood, then a layer of bodies, and so on up. When the mutilated body of Bowie was to be thrown on the pile, Santa Anna hesitated, and then said, "He is too brave to be burned like a dog." He ordered the body to be buried, but in a moment his mood changed. He turned his back with the words: "It doesn't matter. Throw it in." Bowie was, we recall, the husband of Santa Anna's dead goddaughter, Ursula Verimendi.

At five o'clock the pyres were lighted. The end was quick and clean.

It was different with the bodies of a great number of the Mexicans. Here, as in so much, the plans of

Santa Anna miscarried. He had intended to give the bodies of his enemies the treatment due the body of a dog, and to give his own men decent burial. But there were too many dead Mexicans for the poor mayor to manage. He buried as many as he could find space for, and hands to dig graves for, in the regular cemetery. But great numbers were thrown into the San Antonio River—some to float away, but many to catch on snags and sand bars and lie there under the spring sun.

For weeks flocks of buzzards hung in the sky. The air was unwholesome. All citizens who could, left the town of Bexar and its foulness. Among those who remained, there was an epidemic of fever. Santa Anna himself was sick.

14

Remember the Alamo!

THE ALAMO HAD FALLEN, AND NOW THE SHIELD WAS removed from Texas. The country was in the greatest turmoil, and rumor piled on rumor. Sam Houston was now at Gonzales with a few hundred men. Though the government was doing nothing, these men had nevertheless ridden in, in small groups, and were waiting for leadership. Some fifty men had come, too, from as far away as Newport, Kentucky. Houston began, at last, to have an army. But what kind of an army in the face of even the remnant of Santa Anna's thousands?

Now word came that a large Mexican force was approaching. Burleson, who had been in command when the Texans had captured the Alamo back in December, now made an address to the troops to rouse their flagging spirits. The Alamo, he said, was like the Battle of Thermopylae, that battle of ancient Greece where a small force of Spartans had held up the advance of a vast Persian army and made it possible for Greece to rally to save the Western world from Persian domination. But there was one difference, he said. "Thermopylae had its messenger of defeat, the Alamo had none!" The Texans had died to the last man.

But speeches, even with such unforgettable words, could not stop Mexicans. Houston gave orders to destroy the settlement, and fall back on the Colorado River. People were already in flight from the terror of the Mexicans.

Worse news was to come. Houston had sent orders for Fannin to abandon Goliad and join forces with him. When Fannin did start out, he was overtaken by Mexican cavalry in the open prairie and pinned down until surrounded by Mexicans outnumbering him more than four to one. He held on all afternoon and into the night in a hollow square around his baggage, with his artillery at the corners, but next morning, Sunday, March 20th, he surrendered. He had the verbal promise of the Mexican commander that he would use his influence to save the lives of the prisoners. The prisoners were marched to Goliad and held until Palm Sunday, March 27th. On that day, which opened with some fog, then turned off bright and crisp, 390 men were marched out a distance, then told to sit down with their backs to the guards. At this a young man named Fenner leaped up and yelled, "Boys, they are going to kill us. Die with your faces to them, like men!" Two other young men leaped up and waved their caps, shouting, "Hurrah for Texas!"

The firing began, then the bayoneting. When some Texans broke to run for freedom, cavalrymen cut the fugitives down with the saber. The bodies were then assembled. Most were stripped and looted, many mutilated. They were piled into brush pyres, but the work was more slackly done here than at the Alamo, and so the business took more than one day. Meanwhile, at night, the prairie wolves gathered.

The slaughter had been the personal order of Santa

Anna. The general who had captured Fannin had tried to keep his promise, but it was of no use.

Word of Fannin's fate swept across the country. But there was still more news. Two other forces had been taken and slaughtered. Houston was in retreat. Santa Anna meant what he said. He was going to kill or drive out every American in Texas; he was going to make his coffee from water of the Sabine River; he was going to drive on to Washington—not the village where the convention had sat to debate Texas independence, but the great Washington, far off, where the United States Capitol was.

There was panic everywhere, headlong flight north and east, back toward the border. Families began piling back, some with no men (because their men were dead or with Houston), some with only old men and boys. Some went with their pitiful household remnants on wagons, on ox carts, on pony back; some with nothing, not even food. Many were on foot, women carrying babies in their arms, small children dragging at their skirts and crying. Shoes wore out, and they walked barefoot through the black Texas mud, cold now, for the weather was not good. Wagons bogged down in the mud or at the Brazos River. Some-

People fled from the terror of the Mexicans.

times there could not even be a campfire, the rain was so heavy. Many were hungry, near starving, but some people, many people, were willing to divide their last supplies. People fell sick and died. The old gave out on the road. And here and there, small bands of desperadoes looted the refugees and galloped away.

It was the Great Runaway Scrape, it was the Great Skeedaddle. Those were the funny names people later put on the flight, but it was not funny at the time, this wild flight for safety.

By this time delegates at the convention in Washington, Texas, had finished their work and had declared Texas an independent nation, the Republic of Texas. But it was a nation with no treasury, with most of its population in blind panic, with its officials on the run, and with half its soldiers already butchered in the field. Its one force, that under Houston, was untrained and poorly equipped, with morale sinking daily. To make matters worse, that force was under a general who, apparently, did not have the fighting heart. Houston now did not act like the young ensign who had caught the attention of Andrew Jackson long ago at the Battle of Horseshoe Bend.

For Houston fell back and back, stopping now and then to try to bring discipline and training to his troops, then falling back again. All the prodding of the new, independent government of Texas had little effect on Houston. He still would not fight. The grumbling of the men and the officers didn't make him fight. He had only one friend and ally, it seemed. It was the mud that bogged down the enemy movements and slowed Santa Anna's victorious sweep to the Sabine.

No, Houston had another friend—Santa Anna's self-confidence. Santa Anna was sure that the war was over. He would push on to the Sabine, but he himself was not going to suffer the hard return march. He would leave General Filisola in command, and go back comfortably by ship. He had already sent orders for the ship to come for him. Meanwhile, over the protest of some of his officers, he had divided his army to make easier what he regarded as mopping-up operations. The separated commands wandered northward among the coast swamps and bayous and coastal fields, half flooded now. It was turning into a war without glory.

Houston had one other friend—himself. He took the responsibility. Answering an official protest, he wrote: "I held no councils of war. If I err, the blame is mine."

On April 18th, Houston, in what seemed an aimless,

wandering march across prairies like a quagmire, had reached the settlement of Harrisburg. There was a Mexican force over at New Washington, and there were others in the neighborhood. At Harrisburg, Houston had his luck, the break he had been playing for. His scout, the famous Deaf Smith, brought in two Mexican couriers who had been snapped up. From orders they carried, Houston now knew that Santa Anna himself lay with the force at New Washington. And that settlement lay between the Texas army and the Gulf.

Next morning, leaving his baggage train and sick, Houston struck out down the Buffalo Bayou for Lynch's Ferry, where the Buffalo joined the San Jacinto River. The pursued had become the pursuer.

Santa Anna had a plan, too. He knew that Houston was over at Harrisburg, and his own scouts told him that Houston would try to cross at Lynch's Ferry to continue his retreat. So Santa Anna ordered General Cos to join him to administer the crushing blow to the Texas rebellion. Meanwhile, he himself moved for Lynch's Ferry. Houston's scouts reported the movement, and Houston, who had been driving his

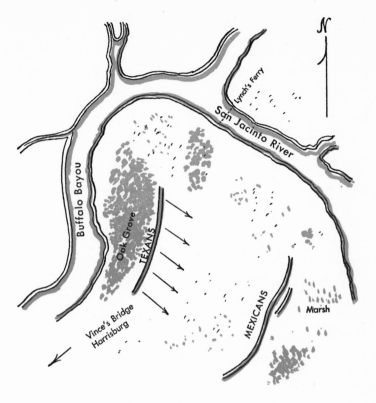

SAN JACINTO

The Battle of San Jacinto

men so hard on the night march that some fell ex-
hausted in the ranks, now ordered the march re-
sumed. The men had had only two hours rest after

the halt at midnight. Now, long before dawn, they were moving again. In the morning they reached Lynch's Ferry.

Houston took position in an oak grove on the banks of Buffalo Bayou, the bayou behind him and in front a two-mile stretch of prairie with clumps of timber here and there. Beyond it lay marshland and the San Jacinto Bay. To the left was the San Jacinto River, to the right another bayou. There was a bridge over the other bayou. Santa Anna marched his force into the prairie, and took position with his back to the marshland and bay, facing the oak grove. It was now the afternoon of April 20th.

Santa Anna wanted to attack the Texans immediately and finish the job. He knew that they were in the oak grove, but the grove was big, and he didn't know how they were stationed. So to feel out their position, he set a cannon forward, protected by cavalry, and began to shell the woods, moving infantry forward as if getting ready for attack. But Houston now had two cannon, and his return fire forced the Mexicans to pull back. The afternoon passed with swapping cannon fire, and then a try by some Texan mounted volunteers to take the Mexican cannon. The try failed, but the cannon was forced back.

So the day ended, with little blood spilled so far. The night blew up cold, another norther, but the Texans got a good sleep. They would be fresh next day. Next day, they knew, would tell the tale.

About nine o'clock in the morning, the Texans could see General Cos's force, between 400 and 500 men, moving over the bridge of the bayou to the right. They were moving up to join Santa Anna. Santa Anna now had around 1,300 men. Houston had some 800 men. But the Mexicans did not attack. The Texans waited.

Finally Houston called a council of war, and his officers decided to wait until next morning, in the hope that the Mexicans would attack. The Texans had their oak grove. That would give them an advantage in defense. Houston was later to say that he personally took no part in this decision. Whether he liked the decision or not, the men definitely were against it. They wanted to attack.

At three o'clock in the afternoon Houston ordered the army to "arm and line." The cavalry moved qui-

The Texans slaughtered the Mexicans. One Texan

yelled, "Remember the Alamo!" Then they all yelled it.

etly off left, the two guns were pushed up to less than two hundred yards of the breastworks now erected by the Mexicans; the infantry moved up in easy range. One company had tied a big red handkerchief to a stick, and carried it like a flag. They knew about Santa Anna's red flag at the Alamo.

There was, strangely enough, still no sign of life from the Mexican camp. At the back of the Texans the sun was getting low, and its rays fell toward the Mexican position. Later, Houston said that he had waited for the sun to be low so that it would fall in the faces of the enemy. He had sent Deaf Smith off to destroy the bridge over the bayou. Cos had come that way. Now no more Mexicans would come. No more would go.

The order was given. The band struck up. The band was one fife and one old drum, and the tune was a love song, "Will You Come to the Bower I have Shaded for You?" The cavalry moved in at a trot, then at full charge. The two cannon blasted at the breastworks. The infantry gave its volley and poured over the defenses.

There was never a more complete surprise. It was in-

credible—in the middle of the afternoon in broad daylight, in open country—but it was true. Many Mexican
soldiers were gathering firewood or wood for shelters.
Many were sleeping in the shade. The cavalry was
dismounted, except for bareback details leading
mounts to and from water. Muskets were stacked.
Many officers were comfortably in their tents, taking
a somewhat long siesta. Many died there, comfortably, on their cots.

It was a slaughter. The Mexicans never had a
chance to form for battle. They tried to form, very
courageously, especially around their cannon; but
the Texans were swarming over, too close for rifle
fire now. Then the pistol fire was past, and it was
work for clubbed rifle, work for bowie knife, Arkansas toothpick and hunting knife, work for the Mexican bayonet seized and turned on Mexicans.

As the Texans swarmed over the defenses somebody yelled, "Remember the Alamo! Remember Goliad! Remember the Alamo!" All yelled it with what
breath they could spare as their arms rose and fell in
the bloody business.

"Me no Alamo, me no Goliad!" Mexicans cried

as they flung their weapons down. But it did them little good. "Remember the Alamo!" was the last thing they heard.

The broken Mexicans streamed across the prairie. The Texas cavalrymen spread out after them. A good rider could do it—bowie in hand, leaning in the saddle—and not break the gallop. For the unmounted Texans, there was again a challenge to marksmanship.

It was a dark bower into which the single fife and old drum had invited the Mexicans. The battle was over in twenty minutes. The Texans began to take prisoners. It wasn't quite in them to avenge the Alamo, after all.

When the Texans struck, Santa Anna, too, was having his siesta. He did not have to wait long after the first alarm to know that things were hopeless. For a moment he ran about, wringing his hands in despair. Then he fled from the field. He was pursued, but eluded his pursuers by turning loose his mount and hiding in a grove. He got across the bayou by night, changed his general's finery for rough clothes found

176

in an abandoned cabin, and tried to slip away on foot. But the cavalry patrols were everywhere. Next day he was spotted; he hid in the grass. When he was routed out, he said he was a Mexican cavalry-man.

But it was of no use. His fine underwear gave him away. He was clearly somebody of importance. And when he was brought into the camp, some of the Mexican prisoners cried out, "El Presidente!"

So they had Santa Anna. Among the darkening faces of the Texans, he was led to Houston, who, with an ankle shattered by Mexican gunfire, lay propped under an oak tree.

The Mexicans had lost some 600 in killed and wounded. Seven hundred and thirty prisoners were taken. About forty men had managed to escape the field. As for the Texans, nine men were killed, and twenty-three wounded, including those among the nine dead who had survived the battle by a day or so.

The dead Mexicans were left on the field where they had fallen, and nature did her work on them.

Later, cattle pawed the bones, and some skulls were picked up for souvenirs.

Texas remained an independent nation until 1846, when it became a state in the United States of America.

Index

179

Index

Index

181